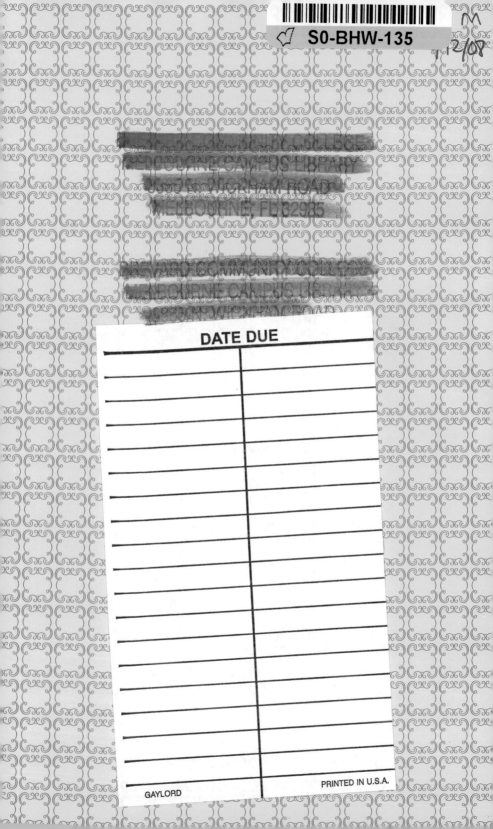

DATE DUE

IN GOD'S NAME

⇔ The Vatican, Rome, Italy.

⇔⇔ Dr. Frank Page baptizing a young follower, Taylors, South Carolina. Ablution in the holy water of the Sikh Golden Temple, Amritsar, India.

⇔⇔⇔ Young Tibetan monks, Dharamsala, India.

⇔⇔ Priest in Lambeth Palace, London, England. Swami in Amma's ashram, Amritapuri, Kerala, India.

⇔⇔⇔ Woman during communion at the Cathedral of Christ the Savior, Moscow, Russia. Women walking in Cairo, Egypt.

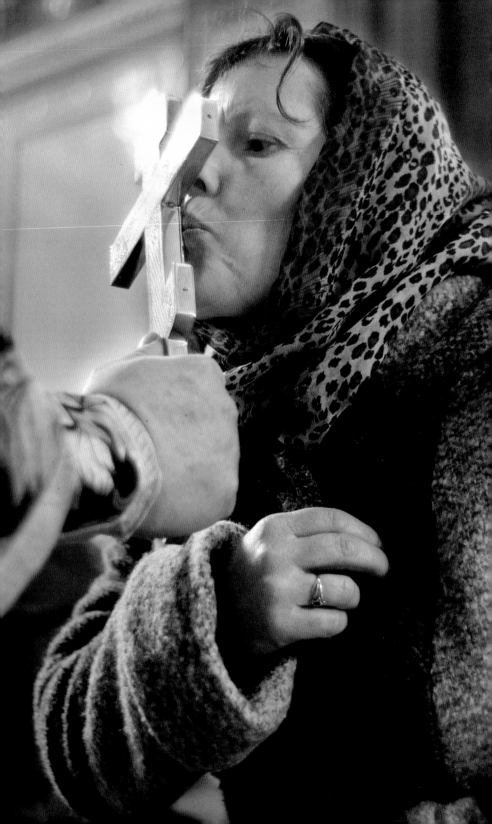

IN GOD'

S NAME

WISDOM FROM THE
WORLD'S GREAT
SPIRITUAL LEADERS

INTRODUCTION BY
JULES NAUDET AND GÉDÉON NAUDET

PHOTOGRAPHS BY
STEPHAN CRASNEANSCKI

INTERVIEWS BY
VIRGINIE LUC

MELCHER
MEDIA

NATIONAL GEOGRAPHIC

WASHINGTON, D.C.

CONTENTS

16   Introduction by Jules and Gédéon Naudet

28   **PATRIARCH ALEXY II**

36   What is your message to mankind—believers and nonbelievers?

40   **AMMA (SRI MATA AMRITANANDAMAYI DEVI)**

48   Who is God?

60   **POPE BENEDICT XVI**

68   How do you feel the presence of God?

72   **THE DALAI LAMA, TENZIN GYATSO**

80   Have you felt doubt? Was there a moment when your faith was tested?

96   **GRAND AYATOLLAH MOHAMMED HUSSEIN FADLALLAH**

104   What is the meaning of life?

108   **BISHOP MARK S. HANSON**

116   What is the meaning of death?

130   **MICHIHISA KITASHIRAKAWA**

138   What is perfect happiness?

152   **RABBI YONA METZGER**

160   Can different religions coexist?

174   **DR. FRANK S. PAGE**

182   How did you experience September 11?

186   **IMAM MUHAMMAD SAYYED TANTAWI**

194   How do you explain fanaticism and violence waged in the name of God?

208   **SINGH SAHEB GIANI JOGINDER SINGH VEDANTI**

216   What is worth fighting for? What is worth dying for?

220   **ARCHBISHOP OF CANTERBURY ROWAN WILLIAMS**

228   How do you see the future? What is your greatest fear?

242   The Religions

256   Of God and Men by Virginie Luc

268   Contributors

270   Credits and Acknowledgments

INTRODUCTION by Jules and Gédéon Naudet

We are documentary filmmakers. In the summer of 2001 we were working on a documentary about firefighters in downtown Manhattan. On September 11th, we filmed the FDNY response inside the World Trade Center. It is there, as the south tower was collapsing and we were running for our lives, that this book and documentary first started. As with people who come close to dying, we were changed profoundly by the events of September 11th. We were left searching for a greater meaning of life in a world embroiled by religious conflicts. We began to realize that at a time when religious understanding and tolerance are needed the most, the spiritual leaders of the world remain for the most part unseen and unheard.

And so we began our search to meet the spiritual leaders of today. We traveled around the world to the sacred centers of the major religions and were privileged to receive an unprecedented look into the daily lives of these people of God. *In God's Name* is a document of the journey we undertook for answers; it is a document of our journey for spiritual discovery. Our goal with the film and this book is to have the four billion followers of all the world's major religions come face to face with the representatives of God on earth and to hear their messages to the world and their thoughts on the future of their faith.

You, our audience, will see—in these beautiful photographs taken by Stephan Crasneanscki and in the words of these spiritual beacons interviewed by Virginie Luc—what we experienced, witnessing the beauty of the different religious sacraments and customs, from the processions of Sikh priests who carry their sacred texts every morning to the Golden Temple in Amritsar, India, to the spiritual singing of a Baptist choir in a South Carolina church. You will observe the Holy Communion of the Orthodox faith in a Moscow cathedral under winter snow, and the communal prayers in a mosque in south Beirut. And you will behold the thousands of people receiving the healing embrace of *darshan* from the Hindu saint Amma, and witness the silent meditation of Buddhist monks in the snow-covered mountains of northern India.

But *In God's Name* is more than a pilgrimage to the sacred. It is a window into the lives of the spiritual beacons of our world. For the first time, you have the opportunity to discover these people not just as leaders of their faith, but as individuals. The journey takes us through the sacred halls of the Vatican, where we observe His Holiness Pope Benedict XVI in prayer. We witness the Dalai Lama indulging in his hobby of tending to his orchids, an activity that helps him concentrate. We walk with the Ashkenazi chief rabbi of Jerusalem as he drops off his kids at school before going to the Wailing Wall to reflect on the day's work.

We hope you, like us, will put aside your preconceptions about the different faiths of the world and rediscover their messages and values through their spiritual leaders.

This book represents, through the majesty of its images and its intimate inter-views with these spiritual leaders, a true testament of the spirituality of humankind at the beginning of this new millennium. Our journey has now come to an end, but we now wish to share it with others, hoping that all that we have seen and heard can inspire you to look with new eyes upon this dawning century and reconstitute the link that unites men and women to the divine.

Looking back at this journey, we are reminded that there is so much more that unites us than divides us in the world, and it fills us with a tremendous sense of hope for the future.

◁ Catholic priest in church, Rome, Italy.

◁◁ Buddhist monk praying, Dharamsala, India. Prayer in front of the Wailing Wall, Jerusalem, Israel.

▷▷ Amma's followers, Amritapuri, Kerala, India.

▷▷▷ Mother and daughter in Al-Azhar Mosque, Cairo, Egypt. Anglican nun in London, England.

▷▷▷▷ View of the old city, Cairo, Egypt. Shinto priest of the Ise Temple, Ise, Japan.

ALEXY II

PATRIARCH OF MOSCOW AND ALL RUSSIA

MOSCOW, RUSSIA

Alexy II is the sixteenth and current patriarch of Moscow
and the spiritual leader of the Russian Orthodox Church.

I was born the son of a poor sharecropper, in an Orthodox Christian family.
My parents were people of profound faith. We lived in Estonia, in
Tallinn, and for summer vacation they would go to the monasteries—the
Pykhta women's Dormition monastery and the Pechera men's monastery.
I especially remember the trip we took in 1939 to the Valaam Transfiguration
Monastery on Ladoga Lake, and the very particular, enchantingly beautiful
northern nature that combined wonderfully with the architectural
monuments: the temples, the hermitages … Visiting Valaam made a big
impression on me, and I never had any doubts about the path I was going
to go. From my very childhood I wanted to be a clergyman. Visiting Valaam
only deepened this resolve.

The upbringing that I got in my family was the foundation of my spiritual
and physical growth. I never had doubts which way I was going to go.
Serving the Church was for me both a vocation and the realization of the
way that God was calling me to follow. In the Blessings it is said that "blessed
are the pure in heart, for they shall see God." The soul of a child that
embraces the church life and the faith of the parents becomes the foundation
of a person's acquisition of faith. People come to faith by different ways—
some through trials, disease, loss of loved ones; others may come to it in
their very childhood—and God gives them this gift that they keep all
their life, and which they guard as a precious treasure.

"Liturgical service takes a prominent place and a lot of time in my life. Last year I celebrated 170 services. Often I am asked where I get my strength. I answer that I get my strength from liturgical service. The Orthodox liturgical service rather differs from the western ones in which there's a possibility of sitting down. The service is conducted standing up."

⇧ Patriarch Alexy II in his office at the patriarchate, Moscow, Russia.

⇨ A ceremony in the Cathedral of Christ the Savior, one of the largest Orthodox churches in the world, Moscow, Russia.

⇧ Blessing communion bread, Moscow, Russia.

⇦ Patriarch Alexy II preparing for service,
Moscow, Russia.

⇨⇨ Donning vestments, Moscow, Russia.

WHAT IS YOUR MESSAGE TO MANKIND—BELIEVERS OR NONBELIEVERS?

Man can truly be a dangerous animal. He can be evil; but he can also be an angel on two legs. He can use the hand either to open it to others, to shake hands; or to form the hand into a fist, and beat, and do evil.

The saying that I think that we all should adopt, with the intention to fulfill, is "Thou shalt love thy neighbor as thyself, and what you hate, do not do to any one."

Rabbi Yona Metzger
ASHKENAZI CHIEF RABBI OF ISRAEL

To restore the link between generations is our task. I think that a lot of problems that arise today are caused by the loss of the institution of family. Family should lay down the foundation for upbringing.

Alexy II
PATRIARCH OF MOSCOW AND ALL RUSSIA

We call on Muslims who live in Islamic countries to spread peace and security. And we call on Muslims who live in non-Muslim countries—in America, Europe, Africa, Asia, or other places where the majority of the population are non-Muslim—to be good examples of Islam and Muslims by being righteous, honest, and truthful by keeping their promises and treating people in a decent way, because Islam is a religion that extends its hand in peace to whomever extends their hands in peace.

The message that I would like to address to men and women, be they Muslims or non-Muslims, is to call on them to worship God faithfully and sincerely, to embrace virtues, not vices.

Imam Muhammad Sayyed Tantawi
GRAND SHEIKH OF AL-AZHAR
AND A PROMINENT SUNNI MUSLIM LEADER

While I worry about violence, I think it is important to reach out to people on an individual level. However, this is really hard to do. That is why we and our festivals pray for peace in the world and why we pray for peace, calm, and security for people both in Japan and overseas.

Michihisa Kitashirakawa
JINGU DAIGUJI (HIGH PRIEST) OF THE
SHINTO GRAND SHRINE OF ISE

Even if a person does not believe in religion or the existence of God, someone we call an atheist, if he dreams of peace—every human being wants peace, whether he is rich or poor, believer or nonbeliever, everybody wants peace and happiness—then the Almighty says as long as you do not hurt others, you will be granted peace and happiness. Those who are jealous of others for their wealth, prosperity, or their children, those who have jealousy in them, no matter whatever else they do in this life, they will not find happiness. These are the principles the Almighty has given to lead this life. If we adopt them, then we will live in bliss and happiness.

Singh Saheb Giani Joginder Singh Vedanti
JATHEDAR SRI AKAL TAKHT,
SUPREME SIKH AUTHORITY

Believers must go deep within their religion to find spirituality. Definitely, there will be a transformation. All conflicts can be avoided and the mind will also become peaceful. Nonbelievers must accept believers and respect their faith. They should try to understand faith. I am not saying that they should believe that there is a God sitting beyond the sky … They should awaken their own feelings.

The sun may be reflected in a thousand pots, but there is only one sun … People cannot live without belief. Everything is belief.

Amma (Sri Mata Amritanandamayi Devi)
HINDU SPIRITUAL LEADER

I think right now we need to stop and listen to each other, to hear the agonies and joys of our life stories. And hear where those stories are different and where they intersect.

Bishop Mark S. Hanson
PRESIDING BISHOP OF THE
EVANGELICAL LUTHERAN CHURCH IN AMERICA
AND PRESIDENT OF THE
LUTHERAN WORLD FEDERATION

AMMA (SRI MATA AMRITANANDAMAYI DEVI)
HINDU SPIRITUAL LEADER
KERALA, INDIA

Sri Mata Amritanandamayi Devi, known affectionately as Amma (Sanskrit for Mother) and "the hugging saint," believes that Hinduism is a religion of love, unity, and compassion. She has shared her trademark embraces with twenty-six million people around the world and is revered as a saint by her followers.

Everyone calls me Amma or Mata Amritanandamayi Devi, but I will not call myself by these names. I am a soul. And the soul inside this body does not go by these names; it is beyond that. What has influenced me are the tears and suffering of others ... I felt it was my fate, my dharma [moral duty] to console people and to give them love. Then I started embracing their sufferings. Because I only wanted to give, I never wanted to take anything from people, they started calling me Mother, Amma. But for me this power, this motherhood or Shakti, is in everyone.

Darshan is a divine embrace. When I hold someone, it allows him to experience true, unconditional love; it can help to awaken his spiritual energy. My path is love. What everyone desires is love. For that there is no caste or East or West, no female or male. All people, everywhere in the world, are wandering about searching for love. So, when they see that sweet water, they drink it; that is all. Love is the same everywhere.

There is nothing to think about during *darshan*. I listen to them and sometimes I become them. When they are in pain and cry, I forget myself and I wipe their tears. Their pain becomes my pain; I laugh when they laugh. Other than interacting with them, there is no condition of mind for me. I remain like a mirror. Just like a mirror, I am always reflecting.

Being known as a divine soul is not like obtaining the position of a minister, nor is it like being crowned a king; it is because they have recognized the divinity in the soul. Where there is love, there is no burden, even if I had to face a lot of obstacles.

"I am always in communication with God, but I also communicate when I do my moral duty, *darshan*. When I console someone, when I listen to their sorrow, when I see them, when I do my tasks, when I walk, there is communication."

⇧ Prayer, Kerala, India.

⇨ Amma performing *bhajans*
(devotional songs), Kerala, India.

⇧⇦ Amma providing *darshan*, Kerala, India.

⇨⇨ Amma and her followers, Kerala, India.

WHO IS GOD?

I see God in the sun that rises and the moon that glows, in the river that runs, in the wide sea and in every human being living his life. I see God in all the manifestations in the universe.

Grand Ayatollah Mohammed Hussein Fadlallah
PROMINENT SHIITE MUSLIM LEADER

He has many forms and all forms. He is many and He is One.

Guru in the sacred book states that only people with divine qualities, and the ones with the third eye of wisdom open, can see Him. We cannot see Him with these eyes. Only the eyes of wisdom and awareness can see the beauty of God. Then they are not far from Him, they are very near Him.

He is Waheguru. He is the ultimate, supreme guru. He is known by many names; He has many forms. In the Sikh religion we remember Him by only one mantra and that is Waheguru—supreme guru. *Wahe* means wonderful, *gu* means darkness, *ru* means light. The One who clears the darkness of ignorance through the light of wisdom. The One who leads us from darkness to light, that wonderful form is Waheguru.

Singh Saheb Giani Joginder Singh Vedanti
JATHEDAR SRI AKAL TAKHT,
SUPREME SIKH AUTHORITY

God is the center of my being. He is the center
of the universe. He is the center of my heart.
He came into my heart as a nine-year-old boy,
and he lives at the center of my heart now.

Dr. Frank S. Page
PRESIDENT OF THE SOUTHERN BAPTIST CONVENTION

I don't think anyone knows God. Moses wanted to
see God and God said, no, you can only see my backside;
you're not going to see all of me, because if you did
you couldn't live. But then God decided, I will show you
enough of me so that you'll know how much I love
you. And that became this one whom we call Jesus.
I know God most fully in Jesus.

Bishop Mark S. Hanson
PRESIDING BISHOP OF THE
EVANGELICAL LUTHERAN CHURCH IN AMERICA
AND PRESIDENT OF THE LUTHERAN WORLD FEDERATION

We believe that each of the blessings of nature
is given by many gods and goddesses. I think
the way to live according to Shinto beliefs is
to be thankful to them and live together with
them. Since early times, people have felt and
cared about the gods and goddesses dwelling
in fire, water, trees, and grass.

Michihisa Kitashirakawa
JINGU DAIGUJI (HIGH PRIEST) OF THE
SHINTO GRAND SHRINE OF ISE

You are my God, this breeze, the ocean, the
roar of a lion, the song of a cuckoo bird, all of
this is God. Divinity is present everywhere and
in everybody, but no one is aware of it. For me,
all are divine souls.

Amma (Sri Mata Amritanandamayi Devi)
HINDU SPIRITUAL LEADER

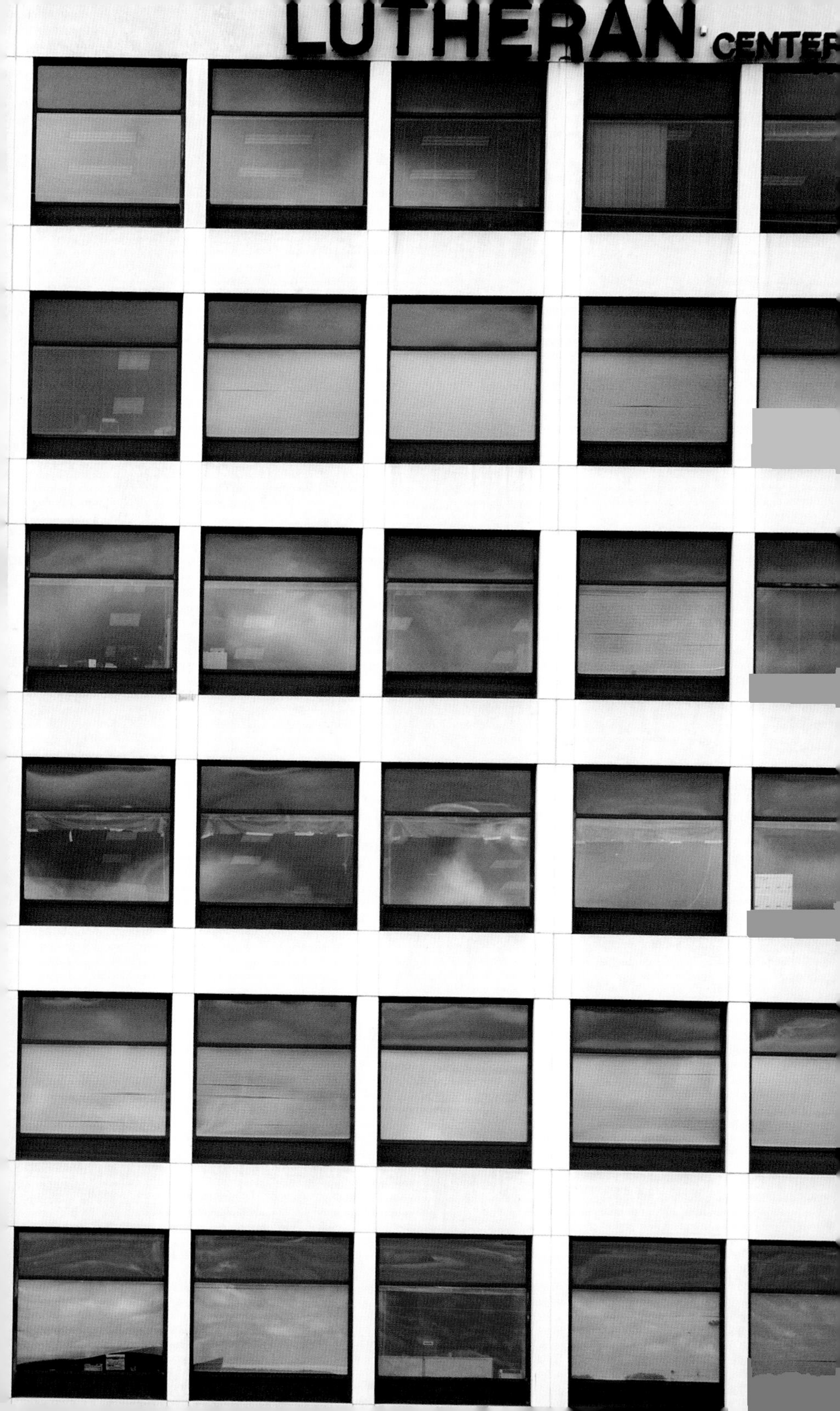
LUTHERAN CENTER

◇ Women during service in the Orthodox church of Christ the Savior, Moscow, Russia.

◇◇ Grand Ayatollah Fadlallah's son and two grandchildren, Beirut, Lebanon. The Evangelical Lutheran Church of America (ELCA) building, Chicago, Illinois.

◇◇◇ Women at the Al-Azhar Mosque, Cairo, Egypt. Benedictine monk, Sant'Anselmo monastery, Rome, Italy.

◇◇ A Hindu man meditating by the Arabian Sea, Kerala, India. Prayers in the Imamm Ain Hassan Ain Mosque, Beirut, Lebanon.

◇◇◇ Meeting of rabbis at the Great Rabbinate, Jerusalem, Israel.

Benedict XVI, who was known as
Cardinal Joseph Ratzinger before his 2005 election to the papacy,
is the 265th Roman Catholic pope.

I always find it very beautiful to walk here in this wonderful earth that the Lord has given to us. We cannot always live in exalted meditation; perhaps a saint on the last step of his earthly pilgrimage could reach this point, but we normally live with our feet on the ground and our eyes turned to heaven. Both these things are given to us by the Lord and, therefore, loving human things, loving the beauties of this earth, is not only very human but also very Christian and truly Catholic. I would say … that this aspect is also part of a good and truly Catholic pastoral care: living in the *et et* [both and]; living the humanity and humanism of the human being, all the gifts which the Lord has lavished upon us and which we have developed; and at the same time, not forgetting God, because ultimately, the great light comes from God and then it is only from Him that comes the light which gives joy to all these aspects of the things that exist. I would simply like to commit myself to the great Catholic synthesis, to this *et et*, to be truly human. And each person, in accordance with his or her own gifts and charism, should not only love the earth and the beautiful things the Lord has given us, but also be grateful because God's light shines on earth and bathes everything in splendor and beauty.

"I forged ahead on a journey that was not always easy. The Lord helped me to arrive as far as the 'yes' of the priesthood, a 'yes' that has accompanied me every day of my life."

⇧ Pope Benedict XVI during the Easter celebrations in St. Peter's Basilica, Rome, Italy.

⇦ Pope Benedict XVI, Rome, Italy.

⇧⇨ Pope Benedict XVI during
the Easter celebrations at
the Colosseum, Rome, Italy.

⇨⇨ *Urbi et Orbi* blessing given
by Pope Benedict XVI from
St. Peter's Basilica, Rome, Italy.

HOW DO YOU FEEL
THE PRESENCE OF GOD?

The Bible talks about the still small voice of God. One must seek daily a closeness with God because the Bible tells us that still small voice is more like a whisper. He doesn't scream. He doesn't yell.

The prophet Elijah said, "I looked for God in the earthquake. He was not there. I looked for God in the whirlwind. He was not there. And I listened to that still small voice." So if a person is close with the Lord and has that personal relationship, they can sense the voice of God speaking direction, speaking warning, sometimes saying, "Do not go there. Back away from that. There is danger here."

So the voice of God is very real to me. I don't hear audible voices. But I do sense it in my heart. I believe through the reading of the word, through constant prayer, and being in a spirit of prayer, we can sense the power of God and the direction and warning that sometimes He gives.

Dr. Frank S. Page
PRESIDENT OF THE SOUTHERN BAPTIST CONVENTION

I'm aware of the presence of God every time I'm
aware of my own breathing, my own heartbeat.
That's one of the things that many Christians hold to
be very central in prayer and meditation. You listen
to your heartbeat and your breathing. You become
conscious of them and become conscious that
with every breath, you depend on God, that to draw
in your breath is to draw in the Spirit. To let out
your breath is to echo God's outpouring and creation.

During each day for me, it's often when I stop,
listen to my breathing, listen to my heartbeat.
I think, "Yes, God sustains me in this." And then in
longer times of prayer and meditation, no voices
and no lights, but a sense of a consciousness of
that absolute other presence quite outside, unlike
myself, which is also the heart of myself. And in that
silence, just knowing that when I am not acting or
speaking, when I'm not changing anything, it doesn't
matter. Life is there. The life of God. The eternal life.

Dr. Rowan Williams
ARCHBISHOP OF CANTERBURY
AND HEAD OF THE CHURCH OF ENGLAND

For us, belief is not abstract; it is very concrete.
A person enters the house, kisses the mezuzah,
and remembers what is written in the mezuzah,
remembrance of the Exodus from Egypt. In
the morning, he does the ceremonial washing
of hands; afterwards, puts on the tefillin and
his praying shawl, and prays. And three times
a day we pray.

Most of our things, the commandments
that we have, are very concrete, and the
saying is that "the soul follows the deed."
And the heart triggers belief.

Rabbi Yona Metzger
ASHKENAZI CHIEF RABBI OF ISRAEL

I feel the presence of God in a spiritual manner that glorifies
God. I love God. I live with Him. I talk to Him like a lover
talks to his beloved one. I don't feel that there is any barrier
between God and myself. I talk to God about all my pains,
my pleasures, my feelings and needs. I feel that God listens
to me and grants me His mercy and compassion and loves
me. I feel spiritual happiness when I stand in His presence
and worship Him, talk to Him, and pray to Him.

Grand Ayatollah Mohammed Hussein Fadlallah
PROMINENT SHIITE MUSLIM LEADER

How can we distinguish God's voice from among the thousands of voices we hear each day in our world? I would say God speaks with us in many different ways. He speaks through others, through friends, parents, pastors, priests … He speaks by means of the events in our life, in which we are able to discern God's touch; He speaks also through nature, creation, and He speaks, naturally and above all, through His word, in sacred scripture, read in the communion of the Church and read personally in conversation with God.

Pope Benedict XVI
HEAD OF THE ROMAN CATHOLIC CHURCH

I feel the presence of God Almighty in a manner that is more powerful than my feeling of my own self.

The power of God, glory be to Him, is manifested in every breath a human being takes, all his life, and in every move he makes.

Imam Muhammad Sayyed Tantawi
GRAND SHEIKH OF AL-AZHAR
AND A PROMINENT SUNNI MUSLIM LEADER

THE DALAI LAMA, TENZIN GYATSO

SPIRITUAL LEADER OF TIBETAN BUDDHISTS

DHARAMSALA, INDIA

Tenzin Gyatso is the fourteenth Dalai Lama. Since 1959,
the Dalai Lama has been living in Dharamsala in northern India,
which is the seat of the Tibetan government in exile.

It is right that other people call me Precious Jewel or Buddha or Bodhisattva.
It is how the people give names. I'm what I am. As for any conceit, I don't
tell anybody that I am a great Buddha, I don't tell anybody that I am a
bodhisattva, or I have a great spiritual power. Whoever I meet, I tell him we
are the same. The same. Had I been having a great understanding, spiritual
power, et cetera, there would be no reason to learn through education
and instruction, no reason to listen to all that scolding from my tutor Yongzin
Rinpoche! On the one hand, the Dalai Lama is a reincarnation of
Avalokitesvara, considered very holy. On the other hand, people impart
education to this very Avalokitesvara, considering him only a small child.
Like any common person they make him listen to the Wang [sermons],
observe abstinence, take vows of Ghechul, Galon. And there wasn't any
exception about this for the one they called the Dalai Lama. Tibetan
people are very practical in doing this job. Then again, they say that through
their inner being they have faith in me and consider me holy. Thus, they
call me a ghost, but I'm not a ghost. They call me a Buddha; I am not
a Buddha, either. I am a human being having all the sense organs of a
human being and a little knowledge about analyzing the human phenomena.
I am also ridden with a bit of laziness. So, while talking to other people,
I do not give any airs to myself. I speak the real fact. That is why people
love me. For me, too, I have no uneasiness. It is troublesome if I think I am
smart and higher.

"Freedom is very important … Democracy and freedom guaranteed by the law, I think, are very important. For us Tibetans, if we get such conditions to dwell in, we won't have much fear in our minds; we shall have real peace and serenity in mind. Otherwise, at present, we have a lot of fear. People coming from Tibet always tell me they are living with a great fear."

⇧ The Dalai Lama relaxing in his
private garden, Dharamsala, India.

⇦ Inside the palace where His Holiness
has set up the Tibetan government in
exile, Dharamsala, India.

⇨⇨ Early morning meditations
in the Dalai Lama's private room,
Dharamsala, India.

⇨⇨⇨ The Dalai Lama at home,
Dharamsala, India.

HAVE YOU FELT DOUBT?

WAS THERE A MOMENT WHEN YOUR FAITH WAS TESTED?

My faith is tested every time I see people suffering unjustly. People being excluded. People being forsaken because of their poverty, because of their age, because of their race. Personally it's most often tested when we've experienced suffering in our own family. We have six children. One of my sons was in chemical dependency treatment twice before he was thirteen. I had to stand in front of a judge one day with tears in my eyes and say, "Your Honor, we cannot parent this child any longer. He is too broken. Will you please send him to some place where he can get the help that we can't give him?"

The judge sent my son for nineteen months to a locked treatment center. The day that they led my son out of court in handcuffs, I felt I had been an absolute failure. The only thing I could hold on to in that moment of being tested was the fact that I believe God had bound God's self to my son, that God had made a promise to my son, that God wouldn't forsake my son even when I had failed and my son had failed. Those were nineteen months of being tested. The love of a father and the son being tested. The faith of a father and the son being tested. And in those moments of being tested, my faith becomes stronger, and my love deeper.

Bishop Mark S. Hanson
PRESIDING BISHOP OF THE
EVANGELICAL LUTHERAN CHURCH IN AMERICA
AND PRESIDENT OF THE LUTHERAN WORLD FEDERATION

Often we don't know how to talk about doubt. We talk about religious doubt as if it were a kind of general uncertainty. You know, in a room with curtains closed, you say, "Is it raining? Oh, I don't know." But there's a way of finding out. I go open the curtains. I look out. It's either raining or it isn't raining.

But if someone says, "Does God exist?" you don't say "I don't know" in the same way. There's a difference between those two kinds of doubt. The one is something you can resolve easily. The other is something deeper.

When I think of times of faith being tested, I don't think it's usually been a moment when I felt, "I'm not quite sure about this or that doctrine in the creed." It's much more a moment when I've sensed an emptiness in my own life … A moment perhaps when I'm thinking of a very hard time when I was in my twenties. The suicide of a close friend. And feeling, "I don't know the value of my own life. I don't know quite where I am." God didn't go away. But it's rather like being wrapped in a muffling environment.

Dr. Rowan Williams
ARCHBISHOP OF CANTERBURY
AND HEAD OF THE CHURCH OF ENGLAND

It is true that the Holocaust caused a crisis of belief in certain Jews, and yet for others it actually strengthened their belief. Because Hitler's goal was to eliminate or to kill all the Jews of the world—from teenager to elderly man, women, everyone—yet we are sitting here, in the tunnels of Herod, in Jerusalem, and while Jerusalem is in our hands.

We came to Israel and built a state, against all enemies which surround us. And during the fifty-some years that we have been here, we turned it into a modern, open, democratic state. This is the "full glass" of the question of belief. Those who stood in line at the gas chambers—who dreamed that we would come to this? And that the Exalted Almighty promised us that we would exist forever as a nation, it in fact does strengthen belief.

Rabbi Yona Metzger
ASHKENAZI CHIEF RABBI OF ISRAEL

Our oldest daughter has been suffering from a form of cancer. I got a phone call from a physician friend in our church, telling me about my daughter's illness. That was a very difficult day. It was a hard day, because I had to call and tell my daughter about the illness that was inside her body. And I had to tell my wife, and had to call my other daughters and tell them as well. That was a very difficult time.

And immediately my wife and I prayed together, and asked God to give us the strength that we would need. Asked God to heal our daughter, and administer to her, and help her through this. And I must tell you, at that moment we sensed the power of God. That in our hearts He was saying to us, "I promised you that I will never leave you." In Hebrews 13:5, the Bible says, "I will never leave you. I will never forsake you." And so we felt that at that moment, and knew that it was true. We felt the power and the presence of God, as strong or stronger than we ever have. And, in these past months, during my daughter's illness, that presence and that power of God has never, never lessened in any way.

Dr. Frank S. Page
PRESIDENT OF
THE SOUTHERN BAPTIST CONVENTION

When it is difficult, a prayer to God always lightens the load of the life's cross, no matter how heavy it might be. I never had doubts in my faith, although in the course of my life, which is rather long, I had many difficulties and trials, but the Lord always helped, and faith always gave me courage and strength to overcome the difficulties, relying on God's help to fulfill my service.

The rough and difficult time is what puts people together and strengthens their faith. In prosperity and in high living standards, people forget God sooner than in the hard times. We have this folk saying: "Unless there's thunder, people don't make the sign of the cross." So, difficulties always strengthen faith. I think that in Russia, the great loss of relatives and loved ones during the war created a huge influx of people into the Church, where people would come with their grief, their suffering, and their loss.

Alexy II
PATRIARCH OF MOSCOW AND ALL RUSSIA

I have lived through difficult circumstances, through many challenges from people who hold a negative view of me. Faith helped save me from falling down in the face of such challenges. I have always considered that all the challenges I face from those who differ with me in opinion and dislike me can be met through my faith, which gave me the comfort and prompted me to pray for them so that God may guide them to the right track, and I never hate them.

Grand Ayatollah Mohammed Hussein Fadlallah
PROMINENT SHIITE MUSLIM LEADER

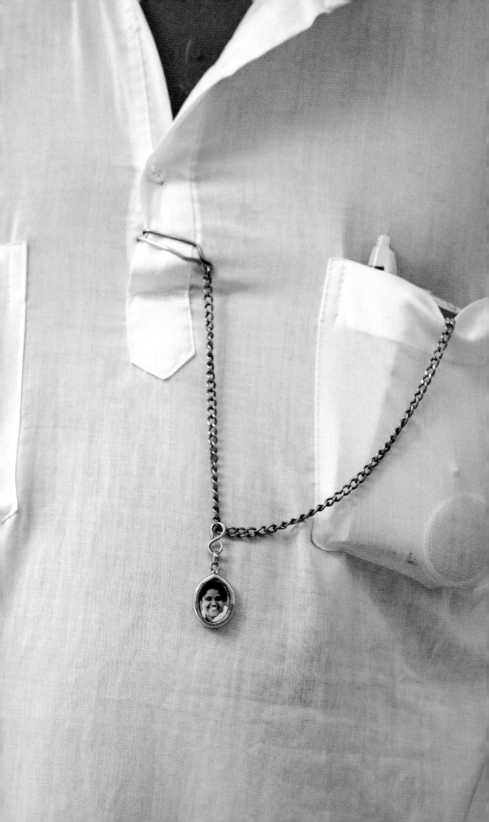

⇦ Sunday morning services at Taylors First Baptist Church, Taylors, South Carolina.

⇦⇦ Anglican priest during a Sunday service at the Parish Church of All Saints Staplehurst, Kent County, England. Hindu man in ashram, Kerala, India.

⇨⇨ Shinto priests, Ise, Japan.

⇨⇨⇨ Clockwise from top left: Holy books, Cairo, Egypt. The Lambeth Palace Library, London, England. Bibles at ELCA, Chicago, Illinois. Holy texts at Al-Azhar Mosque, Cairo, Egypt. Bibles at ELCA, Chicago, Illinois.

⇨⇨⇨⇨ Lutheran bishop in the ELCA's headquarters, Chicago, Illinois.

⇨⇨⇨⇨⇨ Catholic cardinal, Rome, Italy.

GRAND AYATOLLAH
MOHAMMED HUSSEIN FADLALLAH
SHIITE MUSLIM LEADER
BEIRUT, LEBANON

Grand Ayatollah Mohammed Hussein Fadlallah is considered
the leading Shiite Muslim intellectual in Lebanon.

I was born in Al-Najaf Al-Ashraf, the holy city of Najaf, in Iraq, in 1935. I
was born to Lebanese parents. However, my lineage goes back to Prophet
Muhammad, through his daughter, Fatima Al-Zahra'a, and Imam Ali Ibn
Abi-Taleb, through his son Imam Al-Hassan Ibn Ali.

My father, who was intellectually open-minded, taught me dialogue
and debate. He allowed me to discuss with him even the complex questions
which our religious society wouldn't usually allow. He taught me to be
open-minded towards the other and to love all people. He loved people
around him. I learned from my father how to be open to debate and
discussion with the other with whom you differ in opinion, even on complex
issues whose discussion is frowned upon by the religious community. As
for my mother, I learned love and human sympathy from her. This prompted
me to display these sentiments in my relations with other people.

I started to put on the religious dress very early in my life. That is why
I never thought of belonging to something else. But at the same time I
was more open than my colleagues to the contemporary world in which
we were living. I used to interact with the political reality of Iraq during the
monarchy. I felt the pain of the imperialist injustice inflicted by the British
against the Iraqi people. That is why I belonged to the opposition early in
my youth, because I hated injustice by any human being towards another
human being, be it personal, political, or social injustice.

"I never thought that my role as a man of religion limits my freedom. On the contrary, I have always felt that I am a human being in the first place, even when performing my religious functions. I felt that my character has many interrelated aspects. My character as a religious Muslim intertwined with my character as a man of letters and an intellectual, a politician, a poet. I believe that man cannot be mono-dimensional. Man is a reflection of the universe, where all energies mix together and affect his life."

⇧⇦ Grand Ayatollah Fadlallah leading Friday prayer at the Imamm Ain Hassan Ain Mosque, Beirut, Lebanon.

⇨⇨ Grand Ayatollah Fadlallah conducting a marriage contract ceremony, Beirut, Lebanon.

⇨⇨⇨ Grand Ayatollah Fadlallah with a son and some of his grandchildren at his home, Beirut, Lebanon.

WHAT IS THE MEANING OF LIFE?

The meaning of life is to perfect oneself, to be a Christian not just by name, but in life. Because every sin, every digression from God's truth deprives us of the closeness to Him. Therefore, every one of us should strive for spiritual perfection and to help those around us. To try to achieve that perfection, and help those around us achieve that perfection and work on ourselves to this end.

Alexy II
PATRIARCH OF MOSCOW AND ALL RUSSIA

The meaning I would say of all human life is being drawn to that place where we can, with freedom and love and trust, look into the face of God so that His glory shines back. And that means that every human face is potentially alive with that glory.

Meaning comes as you look around and you see all these varied human faces—beautiful, ugly, attractive, grieving, joyful. And you think each one of those is capable of reflecting God's glory. And that changes how you relate to everybody.

Dr. Rowan Williams
ARCHBISHOP OF CANTERBURY
AND HEAD OF THE CHURCH OF ENGLAND

As Christians, what we say is, the meaning of life for me is Jesus the Christ. And yet for non-Christians that makes no sense. How can a person become the meaning of life? Because this one embodies the love of God ... Who suffered. Who pushed the edges by associating with people that nobody thought you should associate with. Who had the audacity to say this sinner is welcome at this table. And this leper should be touched. And this woman should be talked to in public even though women shouldn't be talked to.

Suddenly you begin to see that when this one, Jesus, is the meaning of my life, he's going to rearrange all the realities of life. He's going to confront all the boundaries of life. He's going to cause me to live my life entirely differently if I'm serious about being his follower. And it probably means he's going to lead me into places of suffering, and struggle, and violence of death to bear witness to God's desire for peace and justice. So to go from a person to meaning ultimately shapes the whole way I'm called to live my life and lead this church.

Bishop Mark S. Hanson
PRESIDING BISHOP OF THE
EVANGELICAL LUTHERAN CHURCH IN AMERICA
AND PRESIDENT OF THE LUTHERAN WORLD FEDERATION

We take human birth, first, to dedicate
to the Almighty and, second, to do good
deeds and serve others in need. We say
"sarbath ka bhala," which means "may
all be happy." Not only do we say it, but
if somebody needs help, we extend help.
Helping others is the aim of human life.

Singh Saheb Giani Joginder Singh Vedanti
JATHEDAR SRI AKAL TAKHT,
SUPREME SIKH AUTHORITY

Life is a stage in one's existence which should be spent in
obeying God and doing one's duty and having good relations
with other people, to cooperate with them and help one
another in righteousness and piety, but not in sin and rancor.
Life should be spent in the way God meant it to be, which
is to embrace values and avoid vices.

Imam Muhammad Sayyed Tantawi
GRAND SHEIKH OF AL-AZHAR
AND A PROMINENT SUNNI MUSLIM LEADER

The meaning of life is to love others as we love
ourselves and to serve others.

Amma (Sri Mata Amritanandamayi Devi)
HINDU SPIRITUAL LEADER

To be a really peaceful man, conscious, not having fear, if such there be, that is what I think is perhaps the significance of life. There is no joy if we have wealth but fear in mind. There is no joy even if one has a great name but fear in one's mind. So many of us who are attached to the external materials and name experience fear in mind and live under a great stress. That is why people become old before being old. And they die before the time of death.

The external facilities are no doubt important, but along with that, it is very important to stay peaceful, happy, and conscious. Thinking only about the material development, the external facilities, and not giving attention towards the creation of the inner joy, is fulfilling only one out of a pair of the requirements in one's life. And again, claiming to have inner peace and living deprived of external facility is a sort of another half life. We have a physical body; we need external material development. But we have a mind, and this mind has different emotions, on the basis of which we have to inculcate joy and happiness for ourselves. In this context, if we don't pay attention to the way of inner thinking, our life will be just like a machine; we shall be like mechanical people. We have to be peaceful and serene in mind. And the external materials cannot make us joyful in mind. This cannot be purchased by money. This cannot be created by machines.

The Dalai Lama (Tenzin Gyatso)
SPIRITUAL LEADER OF TIBETAN BUDDHISTS

BISHOP MARK S. HANSON

PRESIDING BISHOP OF THE EVANGELICAL LUTHERAN CHURCH IN
AMERICA AND PRESIDENT OF THE LUTHERAN WORLD FEDERATION
CHICAGO, ILLINOIS

Bishop Mark S. Hanson is the current president of the LWF
and presiding bishop of the Evangelical Lutheran Church, based
in Chicago, Illinois. The Lutheran World Federation (LWF),
headquartered in Geneva, Switzerland, is regarded as a global
voice for Lutheran churches in seventy-eight countries.

My belief in God is the central conviction of my life. But that belief in God
always brings me out into the world, because it's for the sake of the world
that God loves us. Faith is not my personal possession. It's not something
that I'm going to hold on to. It's a living, dynamic relationship with God
that's lived in the world. It's lived with other people. It's very communal.

Religious faith for me is about being whole. It's not about my soul as
opposed to my mind. It's not about my mind and my soul apart from my
body. It's not about Mark Hanson apart from the creation. My faith is holistic.
It begins with God. God embracing me as a person, but placing me in
relationships not only with God, but with other people, and with the whole
creation. So I can't cut up my life and say this is my religious life and this
is the rest of Mark Hanson.

Faith for me always becomes active in love. It's very passive at first,
because I can't do anything to earn God's favor. God loves me because
of who God is. God is merciful to me because of who Jesus is. But once
I feel loved and embraced, then I will love others. I am reminded of the
quote that Martin Luther once said: On a wedding night, do husband and
wife stand there and say, "Well, do we have to make love tonight?" No.
They just pledge themselves to each other. They want to make love. And
so a response to God loving us is that we want to love other people. We
want to express that love.

"I believe religious leaders must always at the same time be three things: proclaimers of the truth, conservers of the tradition, and reformers. Those are not inseparable. As a Lutheran, our Church was born as a reforming movement within the Catholic Church. Martin Luther, for whom we're named, was a reformer. The Reformation for us did not stop in the sixteenth century. It is part of our ongoing identity."

⇧⇦ Bishop Mark Hanson at the ELCA
headquarters, Chicago, Illinois.

⇧ Bishop Hanson at home, Chicago, Illinois.

⇦ Bishop Hanson preparing for service,
Chicago, Illinois.

⇨⇨ Bishop Hanson on his way to the office,
Chicago, Illinois.

WHAT IS THE MEANING OF DEATH?

There are different ways of looking at or understanding death. If you think that a natural thing has come, tranquility shall prevail. For example, fruits fall down when ripened. There is no reason to be surprised. That is what it is. But if you think that something catastrophic has happened, then a lot of unhappiness shall follow.

For those that accept birth and death from the philosophy of early India, Buddhist philosophy included, and accept the doctrine of rebirth, fruit of the good or bad done in the previous life will come in this life. We believe that we get this human life because of the good deeds and meritorious actions done in the past life.

After death, if accumulated merit of the actions and of the life spent in a good way is to our credit, the future life, too, will be good. We shall be born to fulfill great responsibilities in the future. If, on the contrary, we have done bad things in this life—for example, accumulated many sins, or spent the life by creating problems for many people—then different causes and conditions are available for the rebirth with a bad future life.

The most important thing is considering death as a part of life and spending the life bestowed to us as a good life, spending it as a helpful one, and then there will be nothing to repent at the time of death.

The Dalai Lama (Tenzin Gyatso)
SPIRITUAL LEADER OF TIBETAN BUDDHISTS

According to the Sikh faith and principles, the soul is eternal. It never dies. The soul keeps on changing bodies. Why does it change? Being slave to his senses, he takes birth again and again. And also to fulfill karma accumulated from previous lives. He loses his awareness in his mother's womb when he takes birth. Every human being has to tolerate two separations. When he comes out of the mother's womb, he separates his connection with God. When he dies, he separates his connection with the world.

Singh Saheb Giani Joginder Singh Vedanti
JATHEDAR SRI AKAL TAKHT,
SUPREME SIKH AUTHORITY

What happens after death? Life. When you read in the newspaper that Frank Page has died, don't believe it, because at that moment when you have read that, I will be more alive than I have ever been in my entire existence, because I'll be in the presence of God.

And it will be without any of the limitations of this present world. It will be freedom. It will be total access to God 24/7. That intimate relationship that I love so much now, it will only be enhanced in heaven.

Death would be a blessed experience for me. Death will be going home. Death will be experiencing … a promotion.

Dr. Frank S. Page
PRESIDENT OF THE SOUTHERN BAPTIST CONVENTION

According to the Islamic faith, death means moving to another level, another place called the hereafter, where people face the consequences of their deeds during their life on earth. If their deeds were good, they would be rewarded. Otherwise they would be punished. That is why death, according to the Islamic faith, is not absolute nonexistence. It is a death of the body that releases the living soul. Good human beings would be rewarded with happiness, while bad human beings would be in misery.

Grand Ayatollah Mohammed Hussein Fadlallah
PROMINENT SHIITE MUSLIM LEADER

We'll get what we deserve. Our earthly life is given to us to prepare ourselves for the life to come. And the treasure that we have accumulated for that future life will cross with us over the threshold of eternity. And all that we pay so much attention to—the external—that will remain here. Only the soul and the good deeds that a person has done will cross over with him beyond the threshold of eternity.

Alexy II
PATRIARCH OF MOSCOW AND ALL RUSSIA

The meaning of death, I would say, is that it's the moment when we have no choice but to let go. Most of our lives we hold on. We hold on to what makes us comfortable. We hold on to what makes us feel good. And we have to recognize that, sooner or later, we're not going to be able to hold on. As if you were hanging on to a ledge, and you could feel your fingers millimeter by millimeter moving away. And you knew that you were not going to be able to hold on forever.

When we do that, when we let go in death, the question is, do we let go with a cry of protest or anger? Or do we let go and say, as Jesus says, "Into your hands"? So the challenge is, day by day, can we become familiar with letting go? Can we get used to death before death overtakes us? I don't think that's morbid. I think, on the contrary, it's the most liberating thing.

Every day a Christian, like other religious people, seeks to look past death, to get used to letting go, and to practice saying, "Into your hands." … You say that at night before you go to sleep, practicing. Practicing death.

I feel when I die, I shall see myself as I've never seen myself before. I shall see myself in the light of God's truth. And that may not be very comfortable at all. Sometimes I feel afraid of that. I can't control it. All I can do is trust that God already sees that truth. And God already loves me. So even when I see myself in the most unattractive light, God is still love. Now, can I accept that? We'll see when I die.

Dr. Rowan Williams
ARCHBISHOP OF CANTERBURY
AND HEAD OF THE CHURCH OF ENGLAND

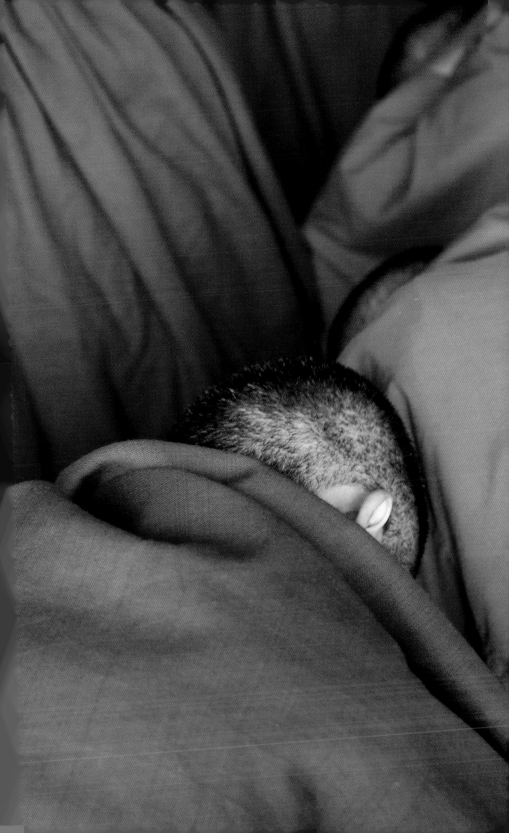

◁ Young nun praying in the Patriarcale
Basilica di Santa Maria Maggiore,
Rome, Italy.

◁◁ The Golden Temple of Amritsar, India.

◁◁◁ Orthodox church in the patriarchate,
Moscow, Russia. Tibetan monks in prayer,
Dharamsala, India.

◁◁◁◁ In front of the Wailing Wall,
Jerusalem, Israel.

◁◁ Hindu follower praying at the
ashram, Kerala, India.

MICHIHISA KITASHIRAKAWA

JINGU DAIGUJI OF THE SHINTO
GRAND SHRINE OF ISE
ISE, JAPAN

Michihisa Kitashirakawa is the jingu daiguji, or high priest,
of the Ise Shrine. The Ise Shrine is regarded as the
most important in Shinto because it is the primary site
of Amaterasu, the sun goddess.

The Grand Shrine of Ise honors the enshrined deity Amaterasu Oomikami,
the sun goddess, who is a goddess of the imperial family's ancestor.
Therefore, our shrine is the one most deeply related to the imperial family.
After forty years of normal life, working in the economic field, I received
an offer just around the time I was retiring. Although I had visited the
shrine several times, I didn't know anything at all about the rituals, festivals, or tasks they practiced here. However, my family has strong ties to
the imperial family. My mother was a chief lady-in-waiting for a long time
and my uncle was a grand chamberlain. My family and relatives have been
very engaged in the business of the imperial family. Therefore, I thought
it was destiny that I take the position. This is why, when His Imperial
Majesty said to me directly, "Please take care of the shrine and the festivals," I accepted the offer. I didn't realize it was such a tough assignment,
however, until I actually started working. I was jumping into a brand-new
world, which made me really nervous. I am still nervous, actually.

If I use an official phrase, the shrine is a religious corporation and I am
the person in charge.

⇧ Michihisa Kitashirakawa at his office,
Ise, Japan.

⇨ The jingu daiguji, Ise, Japan.

"The Japanese respect the coexistence with nature very much. This is how their DNA was created. So it's true that I feel comforted here when I'm in communion with nature."

⇧ From Michihisa Kitashirakawa's house, Ise, Japan.

⇦ The high priest at his home, Ise, Japan.

⇨⇨ The jingu daiguji of the Ise Shrine leading the procession of Shinto priests toward the main temple of Amaterasu, Ise, Japan.

WHAT IS PERFECT HAPPINESS?

When we study life, we find out that it is a reflection of the energy of our existence. It is this energy which fills and moves the universe, generating all movement and vitality. When we study life based on the reality of man and the universe, we realize that it is the arena and space where man can, through his intellect, create a new intellectual life, and through his heart, create a new spiritual life, and through his movement can create new and innovative life.

I imagine that total happiness is the peace of mind, which makes human beings lead a life that releases all their energy and helps them to seek the pleasure of God so that man wouldn't be a prisoner of his own self and a hostage to his own selfishness, but be open to God and the humanity of people in doing what would benefit all mankind.

Grand Ayatollah Mohammed Hussein Fadlallah
PROMINENT SHIITE MUSLIM LEADER

The God Almighty has indicated in the holy Koran that absolute happiness means that whoever does good deeds, be they men or women, God will grant them a decent and happy life. This means they will be living in peace of mind and in security with pure hearts, pure hands, pure conducts, pure thinking and actions. This is the general happiness as indicated in this verse.

Imam Muhammad Sayyed Tantawi
GRAND SHEIKH OF AL-AZHAR
AND A PROMINENT SUNNI MUSLIM LEADER

Everyone sees happiness in his own way. For family people, happiness is in the family, in bringing up children; for those who don't have a family, happiness is in communion with others and the help that they can offer to the people.

I don't belong to myself. From the beginning of my pastoral service—and that was fifty-seven years ago—a priest does not belong to the family, to himself. He belongs to his parish, to his congregation, to his faithful, to his service. And I, as the head of the Church, belong to the whole Church, and am responsible before God for the Church, for its future, for its growth and revival.

Alexy II
PATRIARCH OF MOSCOW AND ALL RUSSIA

Happiness as a whole is perhaps different for people of different interests, likings, and ideologies. However, speaking for most people, the mind dwells in serenity on the basis of the mental discernment you have, the material facilities you enjoy, together with the absence of fear and anxiety. That is what perhaps we can keep in the domain of the happy life.

Being a fool, knowing nothing and staying complacent, and saying the world goes like that classifies another kind of people. Claiming the possession of mental happiness while lacking material pleasure and being poor is also a kind of people.

It is correct to say having external facilities and having whole human understanding and discernment in one's mind ... if the person having such things can stay tranquil, his is a happy and joyful life.

The Dalai Lama (Tenzin Gyatso)
SPIRITUAL LEADER OF TIBETAN BUDDHISTS

Many things would come into an idea of perfect happiness, I think. But sometimes when I have been involved in singing a great work in a choir, I get the sense that perfect happiness is praising God in the company of those you love. And I think praising God in the company of those you love is the definition of heaven.

Dr. Rowan Williams
ARCHBISHOP OF CANTERBURY
AND HEAD OF THE CHURCH OF ENGLAND

Perfect happiness is to be in the center of God's will. It is to be exactly where God wants me to be. When that occurs, the relationship with the Lord is absolutely perfect. The relationship with family and friends is absolutely perfect. True happiness is being in the center of God's will.

Dr. Frank S. Page
PRESIDENT OF THE
SOUTHERN BAPTIST CONVENTION

⇦ Sunday morning services led by Dr. Page, Taylors, South Carolina.

⇦⇦ Women praying in Al-Azhar Mosque, Cairo, Egypt.

⇨⇨ Pope Benedict XVI in St. Peter's Basilica during the Easter celebrations, Rome, Italy.

⇨⇨⇨ Clockwise, from top left: Buddhist nun, Dharamsala, India. Reader in the Lambeth Palace Library, London, England. Sikh priest reading the Granth Sahib, the holy book in Akal Takht, Amritsar, India. Rabbi near the Wailing Wall, Jerusalem, Israel.

⇨⇨⇨⇨ Friday prayer led by Sheikh Said Ali Fadlallah, the eldest son of the Grand Ayatollah Fadlallah, Beirut, Lebanon.

RABBI YONA METZGER
ASHKENAZI CHIEF RABBI OF ISRAEL
JERUSALEM, ISRAEL

Rabbi Metzger was appointed to be Israel's Ashkenazic chief rabbi in 2003. He has promoted the idea of a "religious United Nations" to represent the religions of the world in a diplomatic way.

I am Rabbi Yona Metzger, chief rabbi of Israel, and I represent the millions of Jews all over the world. In almost every country, you will find my brothers and friends.

I was born in Haifa, then called "Red Haifa," in an atmosphere of neighbors where almost not one of them was religious. My parents followed religion and tradition, and raised me with a religious upbringing. I remember my father had to go with his prayer shawl folded up under his armpit and wrapped in a newspaper because otherwise people would throw rocks at him. This is how Haifa was then. There was some kind of "anti" in the period after the Holocaust; people didn't understand how Jews could still believe in God. In this framework, my parents ignited in me a belief in God. Following my study of the Torah, which I completed in the yeshiva, I gradually entered the study of Torah more and more. It inspired in me the closeness to religion, to leadership, to the desire and will to grow also in the spiritual sense, and this brought me to where I am now.

My mother, who is 91, is a very intelligent woman—she knows seven languages and has read many books in her lifetime, and she is very wise. During the summer 2006 war in Lebanon, I came to her and I said, "Come to Tel Aviv. Why do you have to stay in Haifa?" From right and left they are shooting missiles. She doesn't even have a shelter in the house. She told me, "No, I'm not coming. The moment that there is an alarm, I go near the front door, stand by the mezuzah of the house, kiss it, and wait until the second alarm sounds that it is over. And this is my shelter." This is her belief and this is what she instilled in us.

⇧ Rabbi Yona Metzger among kids from
a yeshiva, Jerusalem, Israel.

⇨ Rabbi Metzger at home,
Jerusalem, Israel.

"A person remains a person. I stayed in the same apartment in the synagogue that I lived in all my life, since I was a small rabbi here. And after, as a rabbi in a neighborhood, until I rose to become the chief rabbi of Israel, I did not change my way of life. I walk my son to his ride to the playground or to school."

⇧ The chief rabbi walking with his eldest son to school, Tel Aviv, Israel.

⇨ Rabbi Metzger at home with his wife, Ofra Metzger, Jerusalem, Israel.

⇨⇨ Dancing during a wedding, Jerusalem, Israel.

CAN DIFFERENT RELIGIONS COEXIST?

In the early times, in each place, people lived in isolation from the rest. It was right for them to abide within a solitary religious milieu. In their isolated milieus, it was right for them to promote their particular religion. So, to practice the religion that has prevailed from one's ancestors in accordance with one's own free will and personal interest is solely important. We can't decree that this or that particular religion is the most important. I cannot say that Buddhism is the best for each one of us. For one of my Christian friends, Christianity is the best, and that is the most suitable for him. Thus Buddhism is the best for me, but I can't say that this is the best for you, too.

I generally say that whether it is Christians' religion, Muslims' religion, Jews' religion, Hindus' religion, Parsees' religion, whatever religion it is, they are all beneficial to many people. I feel wonderstruck about the fact that these different religions have been beneficial for millions of people for many thousand years.

The Dalai Lama (Tenzin Gyatso)
SPIRITUAL LEADER OF TIBETAN BUDDHISTS

There is a common link in all religion. That common link is humanity's desire to touch the divine, to understand that there is a supreme creator or designer or architect of the world, of our physical environment, of our society, that there is something else. Humanity has always sought that.

Dr. Frank S. Page
PRESIDENT OF THE
SOUTHERN BAPTIST CONVENTION

I believe that the Christian faith is true. I believe that what is real in Jesus Christ is the truth about God. But that doesn't make me feel I must now force everybody to accept that. It means I'm grateful for what I've been given, that I would love to share it, but that I need to know that other people have come to their faith and their conviction by a route that deserves my respect. So we talk to one another. We listen to one another. We have our convictions. We have our firm commitments to truth. But that doesn't mean violence.

Dr. Rowan Williams
ARCHBISHOP OF CANTERBURY
AND HEAD OF THE CHURCH OF ENGLAND

In every human heart, despite all the problems that exist, is a thirst for God.

Pope Benedict XVI
HEAD OF THE ROMAN CATHOLIC CHURCH

All religions are the same. All religions worship one God. We consider that Moses is one of the major prophets of God.

We believe in the Torah, the Bible, and the Koran. They are all books revealed by God.

Grand Ayatollah
Mohammed Hussein Fadlallah
PROMINENT SHIITE MUSLIM LEADER

One of the greatest challenges today is the relationship between unity and diversity. If we don't have a sense of what holds us together, what unites us—our common humanity and a common earth, a common creation, a common cosmos—then our differences, our diversity, will become cause for division and conflict, one seeking to dominate the other. But if we have a sense of what unites us, then our differences, our diversity, will enrich our lives.

Let me tell you from my own family. We have six children, two grandchildren. I have four African American children, two Caucasian children. I have a grandson whose father is Jamaican. Our family is much richer because of its diversity than if we were all alike. But what holds that diversity together is deep, deep bonds of love and trust and faithfulness.

Bishop Mark S. Hanson
PRESIDING BISHOP OF THE
EVANGELICAL LUTHERAN CHURCH IN AMERICA
AND PRESIDENT OF THE LUTHERAN WORLD FEDERATION

Our sages say: As faces differ, so do opinions differ. Every person has a different face. Do I hate him because his face is different than mine? If he doesn't have eyes like mine I am supposed to hate him? ... It is like this also with different opinions; if his opinion is different than mine and his belief is different than mine, why should I hate him? We can stay friends, each with his own laws, each with his own belief. Everything depends on the religious leaders—on what kind of attitude they promote in their communities towards other religions.

Rabbi Yona Metzger
ASHKENAZI CHIEF RABBI OF ISRAEL

Last year, in Moscow, we conducted an international summit of religious activists: People of different confessions, of different religions, got together. Everyone stood as one in condemnation of terrorist acts, in condemnation of violence, in condemnation of mutual hatred. Everybody advocated preservation of the moral and spiritual values that religion proclaims. And people have to know these values, they have to live according to them, because often people understand freedom as all-permissiveness: Everything is allowed. But there are moral criteria that have to be followed and observed. And in that regard, I felt it, when a big forum of religious leaders was unanimous in its opposition to evil, to violence, and supported moral standards: This is the power of religion.

Alexy II
PATRIARCH OF MOSCOW AND ALL RUSSIA

…ਸਿੰਘ ਸਪੁਤ੍ਰ ਥਮਨ ਸਿੰਘ ਪਿੰਡ ਚੌਕੀਮਾਨ ਲੁਧਿਆ…

ਲੋਚਨ ਸਿੰਘ ਦਲੇਰ ਸਿੰਘ ਜੀ ਆਪਣੇ

ਸੂ: ਬਿਸਨ ਸਿੰਘ ਜੀ ਸਰਾਏ ਨਿਆਮਤ੍ਰ

ਦੀ ਯਾਦ ਵਿਖੇ (ਰਾਹੀ ਮਾਤਾ ਸੁੰਦਰੀ ਜੀ)

…ਕਾਮ ਸਿੰਘ ਸਰੂਪਾ ਸਿੰਘ ਛਾਬੜਾ

…ਸੌਰ ਵਾਲੇ ਹਾਲ ਦੇਹਲੀ

…ਕਿਸ਼…ਦਾਸ ਮਾਦੋ ਰਾਮ ਜੀ ਨੇ ਆਪ

ਸੇਠ ਕਿਸ਼ਨ ਦਾਸ ਦੀ ਯਾਦਗਾਰ ਵਿ…

…ਗਰੀ ਮੇਂਦ੍ਰ ਸਿੰਘ ਜੀ ਐੰਡ ਬ੍ਰਦਰਸ ਰਾ…

…: ਕਰਮ ਸਿੰਘ (ਹਾਲ) ਬੰਬੇਈ

ਸੈਤੁ ਰਾਮ ਜੀ ਨੇ ਆਪਣੇ ਪਿਤ ਭਗਵਾਨ…

…ਹਨੀ ਦੀ ਯਾਦ ਵਿਖੇ (ਬੰ ਬੇਈ)

…ਸਾ ਸਿੰਘ ਜੀ ਘੁਰਾ ਬੰਬੇਈ ਬਖਸ਼ੀ ਘੁਰਾ ਐੰਡ…

…ਕਿਸ਼ਨ ਸਿੰਘ ਸਪਤ ਸ: ਜਵਾਲਾ ਸਿੰ…

⇨ Patriarch Alexy II during services at Christ the Savior, Moscow, Russia.

⇦⇦ Holy scripture from the Golden Temple, Amritsar, India. From a cemetery outside the Parish Church of All Saints Staplehurst, Kent County, England.

⇦⇦⇦ Shinto prayers, Ise, Japan. Easter celebrations in St. Peter's Basilica, Rome, Italy.

⇦⇦⇦⇦ Muslim man at the entrance of the Imamm Ain Hassan Ain Mosque, Beirut, Lebanon. Buddhist nun, Dharamsala, India.

⇨⇨ Amma and her followers in her ashram during *darshan*, Kerala, India.

DR. FRANK S. PAGE
PRESIDENT OF THE SOUTHERN BAPTIST CONVENTION
TAYLORS, SOUTH CAROLINA

Since 2006, Dr. Page has led the Southern Baptist Convention,
the largest evangelical Protestant denomination
in the United States.

In the evangelical community, we believe that there is a defining moment of faith for every person. That every person comes to an understanding of who God is, and who they are, at some point. For me, that was at age nine. I was drawn to the church. I loved the church so much that I would find people to take me to the church. And so it was on a Sunday night in Greensboro, North Carolina, that I felt God speaking to my little heart. And that night, I prayed and asked Jesus Christ to come and be the Lord of my life. And that was the greatest moment of my life. It is the defining moment that has changed everything.

Even though I already knew what God wanted me to be when I grew up, I did not have until that point that faith relationship that has changed me. That has energized who I am. That's given me purpose.

At nine years of age I had already sensed the love of God. I had already known that He cared for me. I had heard some of the stories out of the Bible. I had already been given a small Bible. So it was a growing awareness. I found someone to take me to church, and as the preacher shared the Gospel of Jesus Christ, my heart just burned inside of me that I needed to make a decision, and ask Him to come into my life. That Sunday night in Greensboro, North Carolina, I gave my life to Christ. And I knew at that moment that something had changed inside of me. The Bible calls it being born again. The Bible calls it believing, or trusting, or repenting. I gave my life to Christ that night and it's changed me forevermore.

"My state of mind when I pray varies with how close I am to the Lord that day. That's why it's important that I start every prayer time with a time of confession. Because I need, desperately, to seek the forgiveness of God for not being what I ought to be. So as I begin the prayer time, it is normally not as meaningful as the latter part. Because once I've received the forgiveness of God, and I begin talking to Him, and relating to Him, and sharing my heart, I begin to draw closer to Him and He to me. The latter part of my prayer time is far more intimate, far more passionate, far more powerful than the beginning."

⇧ Dr. Frank Page praying in his office,
Taylors, South Carolina.

⇦ Dr. Frank Page and his wife at home;
Taylors, South Carolina.

⇧ Dr. Frank Page surrounded by fellow
Baptists during prayer, Taylors,
South Carolina.

⇨ Dr. Frank Page playing football with
family, Taylors, South Carolina.

⇨⇨ The pastor preparing to perform a
baptism in Taylors First Baptist Church,
Taylors, South Carolina.

HOW DID YOU EXPERIENCE
SEPTEMBER 11?

I turned on the TV and what I saw stunned me. I thought, "Is this really happening? Is this real?" I also worried if those incidents would have repercussions and how they were going to be handled. Not by myself, but by the world. I wondered how the people of the world were going to collaborate and coexist in the future.

Michihisa Kitashirakawa
JINGU DAIGUJI (HIGH PRIEST) OF
THE SHINTO GRAND SHRINE OF ISE

I was the first Islamic personality to denounce and condemn what happened on 9/11, because I did not consider this way of acting justifiable, both from the Islamic and the human viewpoint. I also opposed those who committed terrorist acts in Britain, Spain, and in some Arab countries. We are against Muslims who commit aggression against non-Muslims for no legitimate reason. Those who consider the actions of terrorists and extremists Islamic are mistaken. These actions are anti-Islamic.

Grand Ayatollah Mohammed Hussein Fadlallah
PROMINENT SHIITE MUSLIM LEADER

The morning after the attack, I was in the street in New York, and I was stopped by someone who was, in fact, an airline pilot. And he said, "Well, where was God?" People will always ask that in these tragedies. There's no simple answer. I could only think of saying, "Well, God is also in those who are digging out the bodies. And those who are putting themselves at the service of others. Those who are there to console, and befriend, and support. God is there. That's still true."

And I had to say that to myself over and over again. And to remind myself that this was not, as people sometimes say, an act of God. It was a decision made by human beings, twisted and tragic human beings.

Dr. Rowan Williams
ARCHBISHOP OF CANTERBURY
AND HEAD OF THE CHURCH OF ENGLAND

Immediately after the attack against the World Trade Center in New York, on the 11th of September 2001, from this place where we are sitting now [the head office of Al-Azhar in Cairo], I, as imam of Al-Azhar, convened a meeting of the Islamic Research Council, which issued a fatwa [edict] that stated that what took place on that day was a criminal act characterized by perfidy, injustice, and aggression. The fatwa added that those who committed these acts are rejected by all heavenly religions, and Islam in particular, because they committed a criminal act that killed peaceful men and women, both young and elderly. Al-Azhar Al-Sharif was the first religious establishment in the world to condemn that ugly and heinous act.

This act, which I described as purely criminal, was committed by people who do not understand religion. They have no grasp of virtues. In fact, these people didn't know what God had allowed and what He had forbidden. They embody all bad qualities, including ignorance, cruelty, and a tendency to commit aggression against peaceful people. As for religions or just human beings, I believe that everybody, be they Muslims or non-Muslims, condemns these ugly actions.

Imam Muhammad Sayyed Tantawi
GRAND SHEIKH OF AL-AZHAR
AND A PROMINENT SUNNI MUSLIM LEADER

Unfortunately, there are many tragedies, not only 9/11. God willing, such tragedies, when people—the old and the children—die, would be as few as possible, and if possible, none at all.

My deep conviction is that a terrorist act cannot be committed or justified by religion. It cannot. If people who commit terrorist acts are hiding, or trying to hide behind religion, they are lying, because religion does not provide any grounds to commit this insanity, these terror acts.

Alexy II
PATRIARCH OF MOSCOW AND ALL RUSSIA

As a man of faith, as a leader in the faith community, I immediately called our people to prayer. We opened up our church buildings all over the United States, and perhaps the world, to have a time of prayer. To seek the power of God. To seek His strength. To seek His healing upon our hearts. And to give us resolve and direction for the days ahead. It brought us to an understanding that we need to pray more for our leaders.

Dr. Frank S. Page
PRESIDENT OF THE SOUTHERN BAPTIST CONVENTION

IMAM MUHAMMAD SAYYED TANTAWI
GRAND SHEIKH OF AL-AZHAR
CAIRO, EGYPT

Imam Muhammad Sayyed Tantawi has been a leading
spiritual authority for Sunni Muslims. In 1996, he became
the Grand Imam of the Al-Azhar Mosque and
Grand Sheikh of Al-Azhar University in Cairo, Egypt.

The function of sheikh of Al-Azhar is to supervise Islamic religious matters in Egypt in general, and at Al-Azhar Al-Sharif's institutes, in particular. It is a job that entails heavy responsibilities, most important of which are to clarify what is lawful and what is forbidden and highlight the shining face of Islam.

In addition, I supervise Al-Azhar University. In Al-Azhar we have, at every level, be it primary, preparatory, or secondary institutes or in Al-Azhar University, more than two million students, both male and female. We teach our students, be they girls or boys, that Islam is a religion that unites and does not divide, a religion that focuses on the good and avoids evil and gives all human beings their due, be they Muslims or non-Muslims.

The fact is I never expected to be the imam of Al-Azhar or even to hold a lesser position, though there were certain things that I heard from other people. For example, I remember when I was still in third grade in primary school, at the age of about ten years old, a visitor to our village said, "This boy will have a great future."

I didn't expect to become the sheikh of Al-Azhar, but it was the will of God and His power which did that.

⇧ Imam Tantawi working in his office,
Cairo, Egypt.

⇨ The grand sheikh doing a noon prayer
in the building of his office, Cairo, Egypt.

"Belief means embracing a sound faith represented in worshiping God faithfully and sincerely and believing in the messengers of God, His books, and His angels. Fortunate people are those who toil for this world as if they would live forever, and for the hereafter as if they would die tomorrow."

⇧ Praying in the mosque of the University of Al-Azhar, Cairo, Egypt.

⇦ Imam Tantawi in his office, Cairo, Egypt.

⇨⇨ Imam Tantawi giving a lecture on religion after the Friday prayer at the University of Al-Azhar, Cairo, Egypt.

HOW DO YOU EXPLAIN
FANATICISM AND VIOLENCE WAGED
IN THE NAME OF GOD?

Terrorism is related to politics, economics, and history. Terrorism is related to exploitation, and also related to economic inequality. It doesn't appear merely because of religion. In fact, terrorists are in the minority. There are about six billion people in the world, and amongst them only a few thousand believe in the principles of terrorism. There is no innate terrorism in men. However, there is innate pride, jealousy, competitiveness, as well as desperation, wickedness, and evil-mindedness. When such feelings become strong, and if there are no antidotes to them available, and one cannot think in a broad and peaceful way, one's mind becomes congested as a result; the mind becomes so confused.

At present, one type of terrorist comes from the Muslims, but we cannot say that all the Muslims are terrorists. Terrorism is also coming from the Hindus, terrorism is also coming from amongst the Christians, terrorism is also coming from inside the Buddhists. But those sections cannot represent all Buddhists, Christians, Hindus, et cetera. Because of this, some people's current description of it as a clash between the Muslim and the Western civilization is far from reality.

Terrorism came into being not because of only one cause. Many different causes and conditions multiplied over a period of time, in one or two generations, and terrorism emerged like diseases get accumulated over a period of time.

The Dalai Lama (Tenzin Gyatso)
SPIRITUAL LEADER OF TIBETAN BUDDHISTS

Islam is a religion of moderation and tolerance. All its tenets call for that. The same applies to all heavenly religions brought by holy prophets. Life since God created it has been a battle between good and evil. Between people of reason and unreasonable people.

My position as Sheikh Al-Azhar is that I cannot muzzle people. I cannot prevent anybody from talking. But, by virtue of my job I would support good talk. Those who are erroneous in their rulings or fatwas, behavior or words, it is my job to correct them, and show them right and wrong, what is good and what is bad, what is rectification and what is corruption. That is what I can do. But holding these people accountable for those deeds is left to security, or the judiciary. After all, God is the one who holds all people accountable for their deeds.

Imam Muhammad Sayyed Tantawi
GRAND SHEIKH OF AL-AZHAR
AND A PROMINENT SUNNI MUSLIM LEADER

While respecting the differences of the various religions, we are all called to work for peace and to be effectively committed to furthering reconciliation among peoples. This is the true "spirit of Assisi," which opposes every form of violence and the abuse of religion as a pretext for violence.

In the face of a world torn apart by conflicts ... it is important to reaffirm that religions can never become vehicles of hatred; it is never possible, invoking God's name, to succeed in justifying evil and violence. On the contrary, religions can and must offer precious resources to build a peaceful humanity, because they speak of peace to the human heart.

Pope Benedict XVI
HEAD OF THE ROMAN CATHOLIC CHURCH

It's been some of the darkest moments in religious life, in all of history, when in the name of God we kill other people. The one whom I name as savior, Jesus, said, "You pray for your enemies. You love your enemies. You don't kill your enemies." One of the challenges today for people of different faiths is to take those broad truths about "do not kill," but make them very concrete in everyday life. That means in the Middle East, a Christian Palestinian needs to say to a Jew, "Do not kill me." And a Jew needs to say to a Palestinian Muslim, "Do not kill me." We must take faith down to the concrete of our everyday life if there's going to be hope for the world rather than despair and death in the world.

Fundamentalism is something about which we all need to be concerned in various religious traditions. I understand why fundamentalism is attractive today, because when people live in a world that seems out of control, when life feels absolutely overwhelming, we are drawn to that which will give us structure in life. What are the foundational principles I can entrust my life to that will give order to life? That will take away all the ambiguity of life? And fundamentalism offers that kind of certainty. It's a certainty the world can't give. It's a certainty science and reason can't give. But it's a certainty that no one can give. I don't believe in the certainty of fundamentalism. I think life is far more ambiguous than that. As opposed to the certainty of fundamentalism, I hold on to the confidence of faith.

Bishop Mark S. Hanson
PRESIDING BISHOP OF THE EVANGELICAL LUTHERAN CHURCH IN AMERICA AND PRESIDENT OF THE LUTHERAN WORLD FEDERATION

We believe that there is one Islam, the Islam that respects innocent people and never commits aggression against anybody without a legitimate reason. Those who consider the actions of terrorists and extremists Islamic are mistaken. These actions are anti-Islamic. They have nothing to do with Islam. Violence is not Islamic. There is violence in America by school students against their teachers or against each other. Also, how can you explain the violence of the Red Brigades, or the violence in Ireland and the violence of the mafias here and there? How can you explain the violence of the wars that the West launches and imposes on the third world? Violence is usually released by negative human situations both in Western and Islamic countries.

Grand Ayatollah Mohammed Hussein Fadlallah
PROMINENT SHIITE MUSLIM LEADER

God does not give any person the right to do evil in his name or in the name of religion. The whole significance of religion is peace: between man and man, between man and God. And "thou shall not commit murder" is a commandment with no exceptions. It is true that there are those who are in a quest of power and speak in the name of religion, with a sword drawn in hand. A threatening and menacing sword. But this is a misinterpretation of every religion in the world. There are people that are willing to commit suicide for the empty promises made by their spiritual leaders, and so we need to openly say that these things are untrue. He who commits suicide loses his place in the next world according to our religion. People stood with broken glass in the trains to Auschwitz and knew they were going to be killed, and held the glass in hand, saying, "If I commit suicide, I will lose my place in the next world, so it is better for me that I will be killed and go to the next world rather than kill myself."

Rabbi Yona Metzger
ASHKENAZI CHIEF RABBI OF ISRAEL

⇨ Anglican nun, London, England.

⇨⇨ Tibetan monks playing soccer,
Dharamsala, India.

⇨⇨ Sikh man studying a prayer book,
Amritsar, India. Archbishops in St.
Peter's Basilica during the
Easter celebrations.

⇨⇨⇨ Clockwise, from top left: Women
studying, Kerala, India. Prayer at the
ELCA, Chicago, Illinois. Men during
Friday prayers, Beirut, Lebanon. Baptist
services, Taylors, South Carolina.

⇨⇨⇨⇨ Outside Amma's ashram,
Kerala, India.

SINGH SAHEB GIANI JOGINDER SINGH VEDANTI

JATHEDAR SRI AKAL TAKHT
SUPREME SIKH AUTHORITY
AMRITSAR, INDIA

The Punjab region of India is the site of the faith's founding and the location of the renowned Akal Takht, the center of religious authority. The current leader of Akal Takht, known by the honorific term jathedar, is Singh Saheb Giani Joginder Singh Vedanti.

I have been granted the service of Sri Akal Takht Sahib, the highest seat of the Sikhs. I was very surprised when this service was granted to me. I felt it was God's miracle. My heart then was filled with gratitude. I was also a little unhappy because of the big burden of responsibility that the community, the Sikh religious institution, and Sikh leadership had put upon my shoulders. I was concerned as to how I would execute this big responsibility. I have always considered myself a servant and a volunteer. With the grace of God, I am humbled, and never felt prideful, that I am jathedar of Akal Takht.

My life is dedicated to the Sikh traditions and ideals—mainly by reciting the scriptures. When I go to the Golden Temple and sit in front of the holy scriptures, I go into deep contemplation and I get reminded: When the Golden Temple was established and the holy text was compiled and initiated, Baba Buddha was asked to serve and recite the holy text for the first time, and since then this service is being conducted regularly.

I get up in the morning at the ambrosial hour, regularly at 4 a.m. unless some duty is assigned to me. Sometimes, when I have duty, I get up at 2 a.m. I do some physical exercises, take a shower, and pray, and then I wake my wife up. Every day she makes me tea. I go on duty for two to three hours nonstop and then come back home. I eat two simple rotis. After that, if I need to go somewhere, I go. Sometimes, when I travel, my bodyguards and I do not even take food. When I do not find time at the office, I let devotees come to my home and meet me. Sometimes they discuss issues and seek advice. If it is something I cannot resolve, I seek forgiveness.

"Since I came here and was selected for duty as a reciter of the holy text—it has been more than forty years—I have stayed in these two rooms since then. These two rooms are dear to me. Sitting here, I do my daily prayers, recite holy text, practice devotional songs, and do closing prayers."

⇧ Singh Saheb Giani Joginder Singh Vedanti, jathedar Sri Akal Takht, at home with his wife and daughter, Amritsar, India.

⇨ The jathedar in private prayer in his rooms, where he lives and receives followers, Amritsar, India.

⇧ The jathedar having lunch in the
temple, Amritsar, India.

⇨ The jathedar carrying the holy
scriptures, Amritsar, India.

⇨⇨ The jathedar, with his bodyguards,
visits a temple in the suburb of
Amritsar, India.

WHAT IS WORTH FIGHTING FOR?

WHAT IS WORTH DYING FOR?

Personally, by virtue of my job and the way I was raised, I think the best jihad any human being can perform in the service of his religion, his country, his homeland, and his family is to spread peace and safety among people. A wise man is quoted as saying that the blessing of safety is more important than that of health.

Any nation of the world where peace and safety spread would have more production and more prosperity. But nations that suffer from fear and terrorism would fall behind and their production and prosperity would be reduced. Thus, if we want to augment production, productivity, and prosperity, we should spread peace and safety.

Imam Muhammad Sayyed Tantawi
GRAND SHEIKH OF AL-AZHAR
AND A PROMINENT SUNNI MUSLIM LEADER

It's ironic to say "what's worth fighting for," because fighting gives the image of conflict. But I think there are some things worth creating tension over—and even experiencing conflict. For me as a Christian, it's for the sake of the Gospel. For the sake of sharing the good news.

Certainly as a Christian, Jesus said "lay down your life for my sake. For the sake of this good news. And for the sake of your neighbor." Now, am I willing literally to die? That's a constant question. Especially as I watch people in the world dying for their faith. The word "witness" for us as Christians also means martyred. But when we see some people martyring their lives by blowing themselves up as an act of violence and war, that's no faithful witness in my eyes.

Bishop Mark S. Hanson
PRESIDING BISHOP OF THE EVANGELICAL LUTHERAN CHURCH IN AMERICA AND PRESIDENT OF THE LUTHERAN WORLD FEDERATION

The thing that deserves fighting for is to defend mankind against those who impose violence on humanity. We do not believe in violence against human beings for personal reasons. We do not believe in committing violence because of political or religious differences. Violence is caused by those who impose violence on you and on all of mankind. We support those who are subjected to injustice, wherever they are and whenever this happens, be they Muslims or non-Muslims. We would fight to defend those subjected to injustice when the only way to defend them is to fight those perpetrating injustice.

Grand Ayatollah Mohammed Hussein Fadlallah
PROMINENT SHIITE MUSLIM LEADER

There is a need to understand that, for us, the halacha [Jewish law] says that we never should attack a nation in order to conquer it. We were always raised to defend ourselves, and that this defense is a mitzvah, to defend the people, my state, my neighbors, my family members, and the whole society in Israel. I thus saw in this a fulfillment of a mitzvah—defending my country.

It is true that for defense at times it is necessary to shoot, and necessary at times to kill, and I as a commander did this. But I think that one completes the other, because a spiritual leader needs to also be realistic. He has to know that the citizens of this country are citizens every one of whom must by law serve in the defense of Israel, and this is an army that provides defense for Israel, and not an army of attack.

Thus, to fulfill my role in the leadership of citizens of a country in which everyone serves in the army, I saw a need to experience the same path and to be a partner with them in this defense, the mitzvah of defending the residents and defending my country.

Rabbi Yona Metzger
ASHKENAZI CHIEF RABBI OF ISRAEL

As church history shows, during the first century, and even in the second and third centuries after Christ, many believers were called upon to either testify for Christ or to reject at the peril of their lives. I will fight for that. I will die for the way of Christ.

As an American, we also believe in other inalienable rights. And I will fight for other people to believe what they believe. I may believe they're wrong. I may know they're wrong. But they have that right in this country to believe whatever they wish to believe. So there are many things as a citizen for which I would fight and die. ... I would fight and die for my country. I would fight and die for my family, quickly, easily. But primarily, I would fight and I would die for my faith in Christ.

I will not back down. I will not back up. I will not back away from my belief in a personal relationship with God that is based on a faith relationship with Christ.

Dr. Frank S. Page
PRESIDENT OF THE
SOUTHERN BAPTIST CONVENTION

DR. ROWAN WILLIAMS
ARCHBISHOP OF CANTERBURY
LONDON, ENGLAND

Archbishop Rowan Williams is the 104th archbishop of
Canterbury, the principal leader of the Church of England,
and the symbolic head of the worldwide Anglican
Communion, which includes Episcopal churches in
America and other countries.

I think one of the most important things that any priest or religious leader
can experience is to know that they are ridiculous at times, that, like all
human beings, they mustn't take themselves too seriously. A child, especially
a small child, is very good at that.

The most important thing that I think any parent can teach a child, the
most important thing I would like to teach my children, is to know that
they are loved, to know that they're immeasurably precious, to give them
just some small sense of how precious they are to God by the way in
which as a parent I try to embrace them and be there for them. I fail again
and again in this, as all parents do. But that's what I want to convey. And
I hope that if they believe that there is a love they can trust completely,
they'll grow into faith, into an understanding of eternal love.

We've always prayed together as a family. We've always said evening
prayers together. And sometimes my son, who's still very young, likes just
to talk about these things. Perhaps late in the evening, we might go for a
walk or sit outside for a few minutes and talk. We've always shared that.
We try to worship together and try to make the life that we, my wife and
I, share, something which is natural and open to them to join in as we think
about God and about the things of God.

"I couldn't begin to minister without the presence of my wife. Although she is a writer and a scholar in her own right, she has always generously shared my own ministry, and made it her own. We do have a sense that it's a calling that we've accepted together. And that of course makes all the difference."

⇧ Archbishop of Canterbury Rowan Williams with his wife, Jane Williams, London, England.

⇦ The archbishop in private prayer, London, England.

⇧ The archbishop leading Sunday service
at the Parish Church of All Saints
Staplehurst, Kent County, England.

⇨ Early morning prayer, London, England.

⇨⇨ The archbishop of Canterbury in
Lambeth Palace, London, England.

HOW DO YOU SEE THE FUTURE?

WHAT IS YOUR GREATEST FEAR?

My greatest fear, I think, in our world is that we fail to see how very fast our civilization can unravel. Both in terms of environmental disaster and in terms of economic and military disaster. We don't understand how quickly it could all fall away. And we don't have enough sense of urgency about reconciliation. We don't have enough sense of urgency about our material environment. And we need some sharp and clear voices to say, "Wake up. Wake up to how very quickly this could disappear."

Dr. Rowan Williams
ARCHBISHOP OF CANTERBURY
AND HEAD OF THE CHURCH OF ENGLAND

What I fear is the growing number of fools who change truth into lies and lies into truth and level false accusations against innocent people and outbid people of knowledge and truthful people. Growth in the number of such fools would, God forbid, spread corruption, not in a single country, but maybe all over the world. As for the future, I trust that, by the grace of God Almighty, and through the interdependence of the truthful, the sincere, and the reasonable, the world would move from prosperity to more prosperity and more security.

The gravest thing is what is taking place these days, the seditions that are as black as the dark night. Here I would refer to Iraqis killing each other with unusual, unimaginable, and unfathomable cruelty. Muslims these days account for a fifth of the population of the world. We have always said that there is no difference between a Sunni Muslim and a Shiite Muslim. All Muslims should be loving brethren. All of them testify that there is no God but Allah, and Muhammad is His messenger. All of them perform their prayers and pay *al-zakat* (the alms of the poor), fast the month of Ramadan, and do the pilgrimage to Mecca, according to their abilities. That is why, in these days of grave and serious happenings, especially in Iraq, we pray to God Almighty to extinguish all seditions. We call on all to renew their human brotherhood and their mutual love and cooperate in the service of their religion and their homelands. Should they do that, and if the whole world went into that direction, the direction of spreading peace, cooperation, and prosperity, if the world would go in that direction, "Allah would open out to them all kinds of blessings from heaven and earth."

Imam Muhammad Sayyed Tantawi
GRAND SHEIKH OF AL-AZHAR
AND A PROMINENT SUNNI MUSLIM LEADER

I wish I could say that it's going to get better and better and better. But the Bible teaches that our history is not cyclical. It is linear and the day will come when the forces of evil and the forces of God will face a final and a rather cataclysmic confrontation.

While I pray and hope that my children will not have to see that, I believe that the day is going to come when history as we know it will end.

Dr. Frank S. Page
PRESIDENT OF THE SOUTHERN BAPTIST CONVENTION

Nobody can determine the future of the world, especially in view of the existence of large world centers, which possess weapons of mass destruction, and the economic power through which they try to take over the economy of others, the political power to pressure the others, and the security power through which they try to topple the others. The problems of the world are caused by those who have no respect for the humanity of others and are motivated by an imperialistic thinking that tramples on human beings' goodness and energy. However, we wish that the world would advance through science and knowledge, which should be used to build and not to destroy life, in the interest of human beings and not against them.

Grand Ayatollah Mohammed Hussein Fadlallah
PROMINENT SHIITE MUSLIM LEADER

If one takes a look at our country, dictators wanted to substitute religion by offering people perhaps very attractive slogans. But what came out of it? There are no more dictators, no more militant atheism that annihilates people for professing their faith. How many hierarchs, clergymen, monks, simple believers were shot or tortured to death for their faith in Christ! In the Bible there are these words: "Will the Lord have spared the world if there were a hundred righteous? Yes, I will, says the Lord." And if there are fifty of them, the world still will be spared. Even if there's only one righteous person, He will still spare the world. I think that there are many righteous people on earth that build their lives according to God's laws. That's why the Lord will spare everyone, and the Church will serve this purpose to the end of this world.

Alexy II
PATRIARCH OF MOSCOW AND ALL RUSSIA

Starting from this point we must find the way to meet each other in the family, among generations, and then among cultures and peoples as well. We must find the way to reconciliation and peaceful coexistence in this world, the ways that lead to the future. We will not find these ways leading to the future if we do not receive light from above.

Pope Benedict XVI
HEAD OF THE ROMAN CATHOLIC CHURCH

⇨ Lutheran minister at the ELCA
headquarters, Chicago, Illinois.

⇦⇦ Women in Akal Takht, Amritsar,
India. Crucifix in Orthodox church,
Moscow, Russia.

⇨⇨ Woman at Taylors First Baptist
Church, Taylors, South Carolina.
Japanese woman near the
Grand Shrine, Ise, Japan.

⇦⇦⇦ Muslim woman during prayer in
Al-Azhar Mosque, Cairo, Egypt.

⇦⇦⇦⇦ Crowds gathered in St. Peter's
Square during the Urbi et Orbi,
Rome, Italy.

THE RELIGIONS

BUDDHISM

FOLLOWERS—WORLD: 376 MILLION, U.S.: 1,527,019

Buddhism began in the sixth century B.C.E. in India, when a young prince named Siddhartha Gautama left his opulent life, retreated into an ascetic period, and ultimately discovered that the path to nirvana (paradise) could be found in a Middle Way, a disciplined life between total luxury and abject poverty. He became known as the Buddha, or enlightened one. At the heart of the Buddha's teaching are the Four Noble Truths: Suffering exists; the cause of suffering is desire; if there is a cause for suffering there must be a way to remove it; and the way to remove suffering and reach nirvana. This way is known as the Eightfold Path, and it teaches Buddhists to aspire to the ideals of right view, right aspiration, right speech, right action, right livelihood, right effort, right mindfulness, and right meditation in order to attain enlightenment.

Many regard Buddhism as a nontheistic religion because of the lack of a central divine figure. There is also no ordained clergy, though there is a tradition of monks and nuns who take vows of poverty and wear robes that reflect the colors of their monastic orders. Meditation is the central practice of Buddhism. There are several main branches of Buddhism, which are divided along geographical lines as well as by different interpretations of the faith. Theravada Buddhism thrives in Southeast Asia; Mahayana Buddhism, to which Zen Buddhism belongs, in East Asia; and Tibetan Buddhism in Tibet and among the millions of worldwide followers of the fourteenth Dalai Lama, Tenzin Gyatso. Since 1959, the Dalai Lama has been living in Dharamsala in northern India, which is the seat of the Tibetan government in exile.

CHURCH OF ENGLAND/ANGLICANISM

FOLLOWERS—WORLD: 73 MILLION, U.S.: 4,870,373

The Church of England dates its founding to the early fourth century C.E., when a Christian church came into existence in the Roman province of Britain. Missionaries spread the faith throughout Ireland, Scotland, and Wales. Eventually the Roman Catholic tradition combined with the Celtic tradition and became known as the Church of England, the centerpiece of the modern-day international Anglican Communion. England officially broke with Roman Catholicism when the pope refused to annul the marriage of King Henry VIII and Catherine of Aragon, and became permanently Protestant during the reign of Queen Elizabeth I. The Church of England remains the established religion of England to this day.

Church of England services can take place in ornately decorated church buildings, and feature liturgical rituals including infant baptism and Holy Communion. There are also branches of the Church of England that are more evangelical in character, focusing more on preaching and personal worship than on performing religious rituals. The Church of England ordains both male and female clergy, called priests, and it allows its clergy to marry. In addition to the Bible, the Church of England draws its liturgy from the Book of Common Prayer, which was written shortly after the Church broke with Roman Catholicism.

The British monarch is the supreme governor of the Church of England. The next line of authority is the archbishop of Canterbury, who is the principal leader of the Church and the symbolic head of the worldwide Anglican Communion, which includes Episcopal churches in America and other countries. Archbishop Rowan Williams is the 104th archbishop of Canterbury.

HINDUISM

FOLLOWERS—WORLD: 900 MILLION, U.S.: 1,081,051

Hinduism is thought to have begun at least four thousand years ago in India. It teaches that there is one creator-god, Brahma, but that god has myriad aspects and manifestations, including Krishna, Vishnu, Ganesh, and a panoply of other deities. There is no single scripture in Hinduism, but rather a collection of writings called the Vedas, which describe daily life and religious rituals as they were practiced in ancient India. Hindus also revere the Bhagavad Gita, a lyrical recounting of a conversation between the god Krishna and the mythical man Arjuna on the eve of a great battle. These writings, along with many other Hindu texts, are in the ancient language of Sanskrit, which is no longer spoken today except in a religious context. The practice of yoga, though secularized in the West, is rooted in Hinduism, and its name, the Sanskrit word for "to join," reflects the Hindu spiritual ideal of achieving union between human and divine.

There are no seminaries or formal clergy in Hinduism, although respected male members can be named as spiritual teachers called priests, pandits, gurus, or swamis. Most Hindu families have a shrine in their home that contains a statue of the family's deity, plus photos of the deceased, spices, fruit, and other offerings that are presented to please the god. At these shrines, and at community temples, Hindus perform devotional rituals known as *pujas*. Hindus believe in reincarnation, and they believe that people work to accumulate good deeds during their lifetimes so they can be reincarnated in an advanced state. This process, like other major tenets of Hinduism, is related to the Indian caste system. The highest caste is the Brahmin caste, which reflects the name of the creator-god Brahma.

ISLAM, SHIITE

FOLLOWERS—WORLD: 120 MILLION, U.S.: 500,000

Muslims believe in one God, Allah, and the prophethood of Muhammad. Followers live by the Five Pillars of Islam: Muslims must profess the oneness of God and the prophethood of Muhammad (*shahadah*); Muslims must donate 2.5 percent of their wealth to charity (*zakat*); Muslims must pray five times each day facing Mecca (*salat*); Muslims must fast from dawn to dusk during the holy month of Ramadan (*sawam*); and Muslims must make a spiritual pilgrimage to Mecca at least once during their lifetime (*hajj*).

Shiite Islam is the second-largest branch of Islam, making up between 10 and 15 percent of the world's Muslims. Sunni and Shiite Muslims divided just after the death of Muhammad in a dispute over his successor. Shiite Muslims believe that Ali, Muhammad's son-in-law, was the rightful successor to the prophet, and should have been named first imam of the faith upon his death. Shiites also believe that only descendants of Muhammad and Ali should be entitled to the highest leadership positions of both imam and caliph.

Unlike other branches of Islam, Shiite Muslims believe that twelve descendants of Ali, called the twelve imams, were ordained by God with the ability to interpret the Koran, Islam's holy book, infallibly. Eleven of these imams, they believe, were killed, but the twelfth survived and will one day return to earth to overcome evil and restore righteousness to the world. While they await the return of the twelfth imam, Shiite Muslims believe that a leader called an ayatollah can rule in his stead.

ISLAM, SUNNI

FOLLOWERS—WORLD: 940 MILLION, U.S.: 1 MILLION

Islam began in the seventh century C.E., when Muhammad was believed to have been chosen as the final prophet of Allah (God), the last in a long line of prophets that began with the biblical Abraham and includes Moses and Jesus. The revelations that Muhammad received and preached are embodied in the text of the Muslim holy scripture, the Koran. Though the Koran is considered to be the most holy Muslim text, the words of Muhammad, called the *hadith*, are held in high esteem, as are the writings that form the basis of Islamic *sharia* law, called the *sunnah*. Muhammad's birthplace of Mecca, in modern-day Saudi Arabia, is the spiritual center of the faith. Muslim men can study to become imams, or religious leaders, and in different countries very learned men might be granted titles such as sheikh, mufti, or mullah.

Sunni Muslims, like all Muslims, live by the Five Pillars of Islam. Muslims may also adhere to traditional practices including eating only meat that is deemed permissible (*halal*), having women dress modestly and cover their hair with a scarf (*hijab*), and reciting their Friday afternoon prayers (*Jummah*) together at mosques.

Sunni Islam, by far the largest Muslim denomination, differs from other branches of Islam in the Sunni belief that Muhammad was the only human being who could infallibly interpret scripture. Sunni Islam is the primary faith of Saudi Arabia, and is the faith of most Muslims in Iraq, Southeast Asia, South Asia, and Africa.

JUDAISM

FOLLOWERS—WORLD: 14 MILLION, U.S.: 3,995,371

Judaism is the oldest of the three Abrahamic religions. It affirms the existence of one God who entered into a covenant with the descendants of Abraham. The biblical story of liberation from slavery in Egypt and deliverance to the land of Israel is central to the practice of Judaism. In the course of freeing his people, God is said to have given Moses 613 commandments, or mitzvot, that the people were to live by as part of a sacred covenant between God and Jewish people.

The first five books of the Hebrew Bible, known as the Torah, or the Five Books of Moses, are the most sacred text of the faith, though Jews consider the entire Hebrew Bible to be scripture. Judaism is a legalistic religion. The history of interpretation of its laws is recorded in a massive set of volumes called the Talmud. Each Jewish community's rabbi, Judaism's ordained clergy (in some denominations, women can be ordained as rabbis), is empowered to decide how Jewish law is to be interpreted in particular circumstances.

Today, Judaism has three main expressions: Orthodox, Conservative, and Reform. Orthodox Jews generally refrain from driving or doing other forms of proscribed work on the Sabbath (Shabbat in Hebrew), which lasts from sundown Friday to sundown Saturday. They will only eat food deemed to be religiously appropriate (kosher). Observant married women cover their hair, and women sit separately from men in religious services in synagogues. Hebrew is the classic language of Judaism, though Ashkenazic Jews, those who settled in Eastern and Central Europe, developed a combination of Hebrew and German called Yiddish.

Judaism is both a religion and a nationality, as is evident in the modern-day state of Israel, founded in 1948 in the aftermath of the Holocaust. Rabbi Yona Metzger was elected as Israel's youngest-ever Ashkenazic chief rabbi in 2003.

LUTHERANISM

FOLLOWERS—WORLD: 65 MILLION, U.S.: 13,520,189

In 1517, a German monk and theologian named Martin Luther is said to have nailed ninety-five theses, or religious ideas, to the doors of Castle Church, a Roman Catholic church in the German town of Wittenberg. Luther meant to incite a public debate over whether "indulgences," the Catholic practice of accepting money in exchange for the forgiveness of sins, was religiously valid. He achieved this goal, and the populist appeal of his ideas—greatly aided by the recent advent of moveable type—ultimately sparked the emergence of Protestant Christianity and its establishment as a major worldwide religious movement and rival to Roman Catholicism.

The contemporary Lutheran denomination is named for Luther, and it continues to adhere to many of the principles that he advanced. Central to Lutheranism is the idea of "justification by faith alone," meaning that a person need only believe that Jesus was the Messiah in order to be granted God's grace and allowed into heaven as a true Christian.

Lutherans believe that the Bible is the inspired word of God. Lutherans also believe in God as the Trinity of the Father, Son, and Holy Spirit. At Lutheran worship services, which are held in churches, hymns or chorales are sung and sermons are offered by pastors.

Lutheranism is the established religion of Denmark, Sweden, Finland, Norway, and Iceland, and it remains a major faith in Germany. Though there is no official seat of the faith internationally, the Lutheran World Federation (LWF), headquartered in Geneva, Switzerland, is regarded as a global voice for Lutheran churches in seventy-eight countries. Bishop Mark S. Hanson, who is based in Chicago, Illinois, is the current president of the LWF.

ORTHODOX CHRISTIANITY

FOLLOWERS—WORLD: 240 MILLION, U.S.: 1,200,000

Orthodox Christianity, also called Eastern Orthodox Christianity, is a multinational communion of churches that believe they are the true successors of the twelve apostles of Jesus Christ. Orthodox Christianity split from Roman Catholic Christianity in the eleventh century and the seat of Orthodox Christianity moved to Constantinople (modern-day Istanbul). To this day, an ecumenical patriarch lives in Istanbul and is considered to be a great spiritual leader, though not a direct authority, for a number of Orthdox churches.

Orthodox Christian theology states that the goal of Christian life is to achieve *theosis*, a union between man and God, by experiencing a number of Sacred Mysteries, similar to the sacraments of the Roman Catholic Church. The Mysteries include Holy Communion, baptism, confession, matrimony, and anointing oneself with oil. The Virgin Mary, called *Theotokos*, or "birthgiver of God," is highly venerated; she is considered to be the most important among the large number of Orthodox saints.

Orthodox priests lead highly liturgical services throughout the day, and celebrate the Eucharist, the bread and wine that is believed to be the literal body and blood of Jesus Christ, at least once daily. Other services might take place in the early evening (vespers), late in the evening (compline), or, on special feast days, all throughout the night (vigils). All services are chanted or sung, and they feature heavy use of incense, which followers believe hearkens back to the ancient Jewish practice of making burnt offerings to God.

Orthodox Christianity is the national religion of Greece, Russia, and a number of other Eastern European countries. Geographical areas can name as patriarch a bishop who they believe is their most respected religious leader. Since 1990, Alexy II, who was born Aleksei Ridiger, has been the patriarch of Moscow and the spiritual leader of the Russian Orthodox Church.

ROMAN CATHOLICISM

FOLLOWERS—WORLD: 1 BILLION, U.S.: 71,796,719

The Roman Catholic Church officially began in the year 313 C.E., when the Emperor Constantine made Christianity the state religion of the vast Roman Empire. Roman Catholicism remains the largest Christian denomination in the world today, and it is based at St. Peter's Cathedral at the Vatican in Rome. The Church is built on a complex leadership hierarchy comprised of the pope, also known as the Holy Father, a College of Cardinals, archbishops, bishops, priests, and nuns. Only men can be ordained clergy, only women can be consecrated as nuns, and all clergy take vows of celibacy. Theologically, the pope is considered to be a direct apostolic descendant of Jesus' disciple Peter, and as such he has the ability to interpret Christian teaching with the utmost authority.

Like most Christians, Catholics believe in the Trinity of the Father, Son, and Holy Spirit. But Catholicism differs from Protestant Christian denominations on other theological matters. These include the belief in transubstantiation, or the literal transformation of the bread and wine offered at Mass (called the Eucharist) into the body and blood of Jesus Christ, the ability of priests to forgive sins through the sacrament of confession, and the belief in the power of patron saints and the Virgin Mary to intercede on an individual's behalf. The Second Vatican Council of 1962–65 modernized the contemporary practice of Catholicism in some ways, chiefly in allowing priests to conduct Mass in the language spoken by their congregations instead of in the traditional Latin.

Though there are Catholics in virtually every country in the world, they are most highly concentrated in North, Central, and South America, the Philippines, and Europe.

Pope Benedict XVI, who was known as Cardinal Joseph Ratzinger before his 2005 election to the papacy, is the 265th Roman Catholic pope.

SHINTO

FOLLOWERS—WORLD: 106 MILLION

Shinto is an indigenous Japanese religion also called *kami no michi*, which means "way of the *kami*," or gods. There is no single, all-powerful deity in Shinto; instead, the *kami* are deities associated with the various powers of nature, including trees, animals, boulders, mountains, springs, and the sun. The sun goddess, called Amaterasu, is believed to be the ancestress of the Japanese emperor, and her symbol is the red sun that appears on the Japanese flag.

There is no main sacred text in Shinto, but there are writings from the seventh and eight centuries C.E. that record Shinto beliefs on how the *kami* created Japan and the imperial Japanese lineage. Shinto is practiced through a diverse set of ceremonies and rituals that are conducted in shrines guarded with sacred gates called *torii* and contain a god-body called a *goshintai*. The *goshintai* is sometimes symbolized by a mirror, but it is just as often represented by empty space rather than a physical object. A typical Shinto ritual is a celebration called *matsuri*, in which celebrants seek to restore order to the cosmos. Offerings of rice, vegetables, and fish are made to the *goshintai* and other *kami*, and are later eaten. Music and dancing are also common in Shinto worship, as is the blessing of believers by Shinto priests with a branch of a sacred *sakaki* tree that has been dipped in holy water. In some rural areas more mystical rituals are performed, when female Shinto shamans are said to fall into a trance and speak for the *kami*.

The Ise Shrine is regarded as the most important in Shinto because it is the primary site of Amaterasu, the sun goddess. Michihisa Kitashirakawa is the jingu daiguji, or high priest, of the Ise Shrine.

SIKHISM

FOLLOWERS—WORLD: 23 MILLION, U.S.: 500,000

Sikhism was founded in the fifteenth century C.E. by a man named Nanak in India's Punjab region. The word Sikh is related to the Sanskrit term *shishya* and means "devoted follower" of Nanak, who came to be known by the honoritifc title guru. Nanak was the first of ten gurus who propagated the Sikh faith. Sikhism drew heavily from mystical traditions in Hinduism (Bhakti) and Islam (Sufi), ultimately emerging as its own religion. The gurus taught that human beings can be liberated from the cycle of death and rebirth known as "karma" by achieving union between the human spirit and an all-encompassing, nonanthropomorphic God. This union is achieved in Sikh worship when devotees contemplate and concentrate on the many names of God. Sikh services are held in houses of worship called temples, or *gurdwaras*, where men and women sit on the floor, often separated by gender, and participate in a number of prescribed rituals, including reciting prayers in the presence of the Guru Granth Sahib, which is the main Sikh scripture. Sikh women cover their hair during worship.

Sikhs from a large subgroup called the Khalsa brotherhood are required to take the last name Singh, meaning lion, and wear five symbols of their devotion: uncut hair on any part of the body (Sikh men often bind their hair up in a turban), a comb, a steel wrist bracelet, a sword, and short cotton underpants.

Most of the world's Sikhs live in the Punjab region, the site of the faith's founding and the location of the Golden Temple complex in Amritsar, which includes the Akal Takht. The current leader of Sri Akal Takht, who is known by the honorific term jathedar, is Singh Saheb Giani Joginder Singh Vedanti.

SOUTHERN BAPTIST CHRISTIANITY

FOLLOWERS—WORLD: 70 MILLION, U.S.: 47,744,049

Southern Baptist Christianity is the largest Protestant denomination in the United States. The faith came to America in the late seventeenth century, at a time when English Christians were experiencing persecution for holding dissenting religious views. Baptist Christianity differed from the mainstream Protestant faith in its teaching that baptism is something that must be undertaken when a person reaches an "age of reason" and decides to make a personal commitment to Jesus Christ as his or her savior, rather than the traditional practice of baptism being performed at infancy to secure a soul's place in heaven. Baptists also believe in "the priesthood of all believers," meaning that individual Christians can petition God and interpret scripture on their own, without the intercession of a member of the clergy.

Today's Southern Baptists are among many Baptist denominations in the United States who continue to adhere to these core beliefs, practicing adult baptism by completely immersing the believer in water. Southern Baptist worship services are not highly liturgical or ritualistic, and they usually feature hymns, a sermon, and an altar call, during which attendees are invited to come forward and declare their decision to become baptized Christians. Southern Baptists are theologically conservative, believing that the Bible is the literal, inerrant word of God and ordaining only men to pastoral office.

Though each Southern Baptist congregation is independent, the Southern Baptist Convention meets annually to discuss and debate matters of doctrine, teaching, and theology that are published in the Baptist Faith & Message, a document that was last revised in 2000. The president of the Southern Baptist Convention is the Reverend Dr. Frank S. Page.

OF GOD AND MEN BY VIRGINIE LUC

When Jules and Gédéon Naudet invited me to participate in this project and work with them to interview twelve of the world's great spiritual leaders, it felt immediately like a meaningful and humbling project.

Why did we embark upon such a journey? What were we looking for in the shadow of prayers and the light of the wise? Approaching religious men and women seemed a religious act in itself, linking us to something greater than ourselves.

For two hundred years, people have been announcing the end of religion in the modern world. Religion has been accused of being a form of intellectual, psychological, and socioeconomic alienation, an obstacle to individual and collective progress. Science, critical reason, and self-awareness were the keys to a better world, a world in which mankind would at last be free from the shackles of religious illusion. But in its attempts to eradicate "religious myth," modern society has developed a new myth to replace the old one: the myth of progress.

This promise of an ever more radiant future achieved by dint of political, scientific, and technological progress has been undermined by a series of catastrophes in the twentieth century. Communism, materialism, and psychoanalysis failed to deliver. Faith in progress and the hopes placed in "civilization" evaporated, vaporized by the Second World War and its millions of fatalities; by Hiroshima, the Gulag, and the Shoah; as well as by the genocides in Rwanda, Tibet, and Sudan. Paradoxically, as these horrors have swept the world, human beings have reinforced their links and ties with the spiritual universe. At the beginning of the twentieth century, 50 percent of the world's population claimed to belong to one of the four major religions—Catholicism, Protestantism, Islam, and Hinduism. Today, at the start of the twenty-first century, the figure is 64 percent. And some experts predict that it will rise to 70 percent by 2025.

For good or ill, the world's religions are in a healthy state. Religion is alive for the Hindu Amma who in her embrace delivers a universal maternal love, as well as for the extremists who, in the name of Allah, fly aircraft into skyscrapers. But God should never be confused with what men make of him. Since the dawn of time, the history of religion has been inextricably linked to war and bloodshed. Religion has been used as a pretext for all types of fanaticism. It excites as much as it calms, stirs up as much as it quells.

The man of God is no longer cut off from the world. He may be the one who controls the blinding light and the frightening shadow, everything that has to do with the supra-world, but he is no longer the force that dulls the masses' minds. On the contrary, at a time when religion is returning in strength, spiritual leaders possess a formidable power, a power not to be entrusted into just any hands.

Beyond history, beyond the multitude of events and power-wielding men and women, beyond the inexorable succession of happenings inscribed in the stones of time, there is the immutable. Religion has nothing to do with the changeable fancies of fashion. For an Indian, the Ganges is always the Ganges. For an American farmer, Christ is always the man who, one stormy day at Golgotha, was crucified. Today, the men and women of God bear witness. Whether the unquestioned spiritual guide of a million souls, like Pope Benedict XVI, or a divine soul who has suffered human violence, like the Dalai Lama, these people are the guardians of a vast interior empire, where time is of no importance and the values are different from those of the earthly realm. In the interviews we conducted with these twelve great spiritual leaders, it is this empire through which we have journeyed.

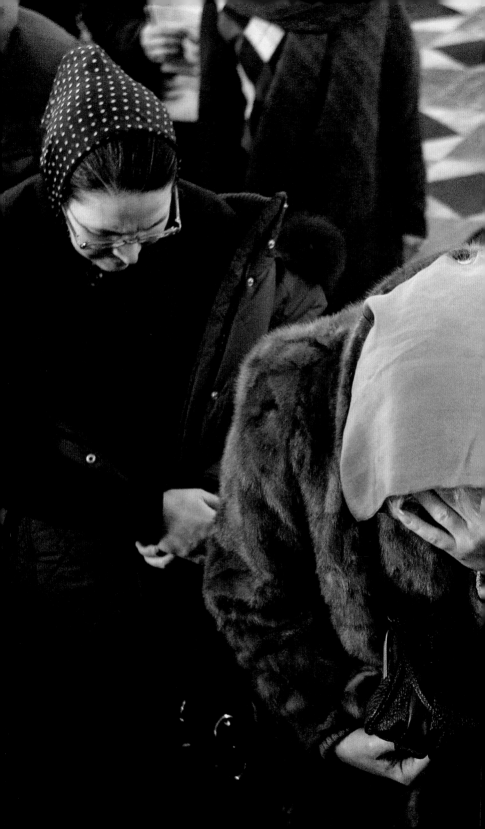

◁ Muslim man at mosque,
Beirut, Lebanon.

◁◁ Shinto priests at the Grand Shrine,
Ise, Japan.

◁◁◁ Russian Orthodox parishioners
in the Cathedral of Christ the Savior,
Moscow, Russia.

◁▷ View of Jerusalem from the Mount
of Olives, Jerusalem, Israel.

◁▷▷ Hindu woman in prayer,
Kerala, India.

CONTRIBUTORS

Award-winning documentary filmmakers JULES and GÉDÉON NAUDET released their first feature-length documentary, *Hope, Gloves, and Redemption*, in 2000. The film was awarded grand-jury honors at the 2000 New York Independent Film and Video Festival. Their widely acclaimed second documentary, *9/11*, was introduced by Robert De Niro and aired on the six-month, one-year, and five-year anniversaries of September 11. It was shown simultaneously in more than one hundred countries and won the 2002 Emmy for Best Documentary, the Peabody Award, and the Edward R. Murrow Award. The film helped raise more than $2 million for the families of firefighters.

VIRGINIE LUC is a journalist and essayist. She has conducted exclusive interviews with major people of our time, from Pope John Paul II to President H. Mubarak, from Stephen Hawking to Bill Gates, from the artists Roy Lichtenstein, Robert Rauschenberg, and Andres Serrano to the greatest athletes, and has been published in *Life*, *Time*, *Newsweek*, *Sports Illustrated*, *Paris Match*, and the *Sunday Times*. Her essays on religion, athletes, art, and literature have been published throughout Europe and the United States. She is the executive coproducer and coauthor of *In God's Name*.

STEPHAN CRASNEANSCKI recently completed a series of portraits of twenty-five contemporary artists, including Yoko Ono, Sophie Calle, Stephen Shore, and Nobuyoshi Araki, as part of an upcoming exhibition sponsored by Chanel. In 2000, he founded Soundwalk—cutting-edge audio guides that allow listeners to experience a city and neighborhood as insiders. Soundwalk has won Audie Awards for Best Original Work and received the prestigious Dalton Pen Award for its Sonic Memorial Soundwalk of Ground Zero, narrated by Paul Auster. The New York and Paris Soundwalks were recently adapted into a series of films for television.

CREDITS AND ACKNOWLEDGMENTS

Author Acknowledgments
Thanks to Mr. Bakir, Mr. Hossam Labid, and Mohammad Sakr in Egypt;
Eugene Correa, Mejindarpal Kaur, Kuldip Singh, United Sikhs, Swami
Amritaswarupananda, Swami Amriteswaryai, Gautam Harvey, Vinay Marshall,
Fouad Nassif, Swami Ramakrishnananda Puri, Rob Sidon, Sonam Gyatso, Dechen
Namgyal Maja, and Tenzin Taklha in India; Orit Mashmush, Ofra Metzger, and
Rabbi Eliahou Shamoula in Israel; Ikuko Yamashita in Japan; Sheikh Hassan
Bashir, Etienne Druilhe (Livingstone), Omar Ali Grant Al-Khoei Foundation, and
Ghassan Rimlawi in Lebanon; Father Abramov, Father Vsevolod Chaplin, Mikhail
Moiseev, and Father Mikhail Prokopenko in Russia; Reverend Jonathan Jennings,
Marie Papworth, and Jane Williams in the United Kingdom; Ione Hanson,
Ava Martin, Larry Bateman, Ari Goldman, Diann Greer, Sherrie Holt, Kim Keller,
Renee Morton, Allison Page, Dayle Page, and Melissa Page Strange in the United
States; Marco Alpigiani, Costanza Barone, Cardinal John P. Foley, Father Federico
Lombardi, Roberto Romolo, and Dr. Angelo Scelzo at the Vatican.

Thanks also to Reveille LLc, Chris Grant, Melissa Leffler, Dave Meyer, John Pollak,
Eli Shibley, Frankfurt Kurnit Klein & Selz, Lisa E.Davis, Esq., Rob Pellechia, Abel
Cine Tech, Peter Abel, Matt Porwoll, Taylor & Taylor Associates, Inc., Bridget Hickey,
and Jon and Anne Abbott.

Many thanks to Yann Battefort, Jerome Bonnafont, Susan Bennett, Sandrine
Butteau, Ric Burns, Rusty Dalal, Francois Delattre, David Fahey, David Friend,
Richard Gere, Alain Genestar, Simon Gurney at BBC Worldwide, Mathilde, Louis
& Jean-Christophe Grangé, Cecilia Harvey at Universal Publishing, Danièle Luc,
Asa Mader, David McCleery, Nicole and Michele Moulin, Jacqueline Naudet,
Jean-Jacques and Shiva Naudet, Siegfried Paquet, Gerard Rancinan, Jane Root,
Regis le Sommier, Buddy Squire, Zehra Tharoo at Islamic Centre of England,
and Dug Winningham.

Thank you to Paul Barrois, our producer; Bérénice Debras, our researcher who
directed us around the world from Paris; and Michael Lavin in the UK for his
help with translation.

Special thanks also to Laurent Attias, whose tireless work made this book possible;
and Leslie Moonves, Mark Koops, and Ben Silverman for always believing in us.

Melcher Media would also like to thank David E. Brown, John Clifford,
Daniel del Valle, Susan Hitchcock, Kevin Mulroy, Lauren Nathan, Lia Ronnen,
Holly Lebowitz Rossi, Holly Rothman, Jessi Rymill, Lindsey Stanberry,
Iris Sutcliffe, Herb Thornby, Diana Varvara, and Megan Worman.

This book was produced by

MELCHER
MEDIA

Melcher Media, Inc.
124 West 13th Street, New York, NY 10011
www.melcher.com

Publisher: Charles Melcher
Associate Publisher: Bonnie Eldon
Editor in Chief: Duncan Bock
Project Editor: Betty Wong
Associate Editor: Shoshana Thaler
Production Director: Kurt Andrews

Additional text on religions by Holly Lebowitz Rossi

Photographs edited with Laurent Attias

Photographic printing: Jon & Anne Abbott, NYC

Design: Think Studio, NYC

Published by the National Geographic Society
John M. Fahey Jr., President and Chief Executive Officer
Gilbert M. Grosvenor, Chairman of the Board
Tim T. Kelly, President, Global Media Group
Nina D. Hoffman, Executive Vice President; President, Book Publishing Group

Prepared by the Book Division
Kevin Mulroy, Senior Vice President and Publisher
Susan Tyler Hitchcock, Project Editor

In God's Name
Introduction by Jules and Gédéon Naudet
Photographs by Stephan Crasneanscki
Interviews by Virginie Luc

Founded in 1888, the National Geographic Society is one of the largest nonprofit scientific and educational organizations in the world. It reaches more than 285 million people worldwide each month through its official journal, NATIONAL GEOGRAPHIC, and its four other magazines; the National Geographic Channel; television documentaries; radio programs; films; books; videos and DVDs; maps; and interactive media. National Geographic has funded more than 8,000 scientific research projects and supports an education program combating geographic illiteracy.

For more information, please call
1-800-NGS LINE (647-5463)
or write to the following address:

National Geographic Society
1145 17th Street N.W.
Washington, D.C. 20036-4688 U.S.A.

Visit us online at
www.nationalgeographic.com/books

For information about special discounts for bulk purchases,
please contact National Geographic Books Special Sales:
ngspecsales@ngs.org

For rights or permissions inquiries, please contact National Geographic Books
Subsidiary Rights: ngbookrights@ngs.org

Library of Congress Cataloging-in-Publication Data is on file with the publisher.
ISBN 978-1-4262-0383-1

Printed in Hong Kong.